C000200894

MURDERS
IN THE WINNATS PASS

MURDERS
IN THE WINNATS PASS

MARK HENDERSON

AMBERLEY

First published 2010

Amberley Publishing Plc
Cirencester Road, Chalford,
Stroud, Gloucestershire, GL6 8PE

www.amberley-books.com

Copyright © Mark Henderson 2010

The right of Mark Henderson to be identified as the Author
of this work has been asserted in accordance with the
Copyrights, Designs and Patents Act 1988.

All rights reserved. No part of this book may be reprinted
or reproduced or utilised in any form or by any electronic,
mechanical or other means, now known or hereafter invented,
including photocopying and recording, or in any information
storage or retrieval system, without the permission in writing
from the Publishers.

British Library Cataloguing in Publication Data.
A catalogue record for this book is available from the British
Library.

ISBN 978-1-4456-0014-7

Typeset in 10pt on 12pt Sabon.
Typesetting and Origination by Fonthill.
Printed in the UK.

Contents

Foreword 7

1 The Story in its Geographical and Cultural Setting 11

2. The Earliest Written Account 37

3 Other Early Variants 53

4 The Wood Version 72

5 Later Developments of the Tale 94

6 Historical Aspects 115

7 The Winnats Pass Murder Story as an 'Evolving Legend' 132

Appendix I

Newspaper Accounts of the Winnats Pass Murders 151

Appendix II

The Diary of Edward Bagshawe (1690-1769) 158

Endnotes 165

References 178

Chantrey engraving, 'View of Hope Dale from the Winnats'.

Foreword

When you tell a story – anecdote, joke, rumour, historical vignette, news report, etc. – it differs from the version you heard or read. It is differently worded, and names, dates, locations etc. may also be changed. Reconstruction from memory alters the narrative. Sometimes the alterations are deliberate: inventive raconteurs add details that are likely to please a particular audience or convey a particular message – or, alternatively, omit or modify elements that could offend the audience or obscure the message. Thus, both memory and creativity ensure that stories mutate between hearing (or reading) and reciting. You never tell any story twice in exactly the same way, and someone else may tell it quite differently. Oral transmission generates variants.

Since folktales, including legends, are stories that pass orally from teller to teller and have no 'authentic' or 'definitive' versions, it follows that they all exist in several variant forms. Variants also arise among written adaptations, as in the urban legends and jokes that circulate nowadays via the internet, changing repeatedly during their electronic travels. No matter whether they are spoken, written in books or transmitted by e-mail, and no matter whether they are purely fictitious or based on alleged historical events, folktales evolve. The mechanism by which they evolve is a matter of considerable interest.

The Derbyshire Peak District abounds in folktales. One of the best-known is a legend about a young couple who were supposedly murdered by local lead miners while travelling through the area. The incident is said to have occurred during the mid-eighteenth century at one of the most picturesque locations in the Peak District, now a favourite tourist destination: the Winnats Pass near Castleton. The story is held to be essentially 'true' (i.e. a matter of historical fact), though most modern versions contain imaginary and sometimes inconsistent features. The earliest known account dates from 1785, apparently within living memory of the murders, and new ones are now published almost every year in books and online. Because so many written variants have been preserved over a period of more than two centuries, the story of the murders in the Winnats Pass provides an unusually clear illustration of the way in which a folktale can evolve in a developed, industrialised, increasingly literate culture such as post-1750 Britain.

But for that very reason it presents a conundrum. Robberies and murders by footpads were commonplace in the eighteenth century even on the well-travelled highways of southern England, let alone in an area that was then wild, remote and seldom visited by outsiders. Many murders are known to have been committed within a few miles of Castleton in the eighteenth and early nineteenth centuries. The victims included a 'Scottish' peddler in Stoney Middleton, a young man called William Wood (not the historian of that name) who was robbed and killed by three men near Whaley Bridge, and Hannah Oliver, the toll-keeper on the turnpike road at Wardlow Mires. (Anthony Lingard, who was found guilty of the Hannah Oliver murder, became the last man in the area to be gibbeted.) There were numerous other reported cases, and many more must have gone unrecorded. Such tales often feature in local collections, but the story of the Winnats Pass murders is better known than any of them. It appears in local guidebooks, textbooks and technical papers as well as almost all Peak District folklore anthologies. Why did this particular instance of an everyday and even banal crime give rise to a legend that has proved so enduring and gained such widespread popularity; and why was it first written down in 1785, two generations before there was any significant attempt to record Derbyshire folklore – or local history?

Those questions struck me when I began to trace the early variants of the tale, and my attempts to answer them led to this book. An obvious line of investigation was the environment in which the story was born and raised: the eighteenth and nineteenth century Peak District, particularly eighteenth century Castleton. I unearthed relevant information from libraries, archives, parish registers and other sources, but that led to further questions concerning – for example – the early history of Methodism in the area, the forerunners of Peak District tourism, the construction of turnpike roads, and the Romantic Movement. I found new insights into local history as well as the evolution of the legend *per se*. Although I cannot answer the most frequently asked question about the Winnats Pass murders – who were the victims? – the inquiry proved fruitful. The juxtaposition and interlocking of folklore research with local history made the 'story of the story' fascinating and surprising. This book tells it.

While I was researching the subject I received a good deal of expert help and advice, though it goes without saying that my informants are not responsible for any errors I may have committed. I particularly wish to thank the following. Peter Harrison of the Castleton Historical Society provided me with a wealth of local knowledge and a number of photocopies of valuable articles that I would have otherwise missed. My discussions with Peter and his wife, Anne, proved a recurrent source of inspiration. In particular, Peter lent me not only a copy of his own book on the history of Castleton but also the excellent study by Roger Flindall, which includes the most scholarly analysis (by some distance) of the Winnats Pass murders hitherto published. Roger's article alerted me to a number of sources of which I had previously been unaware, including Hannah Wright's notebook of 1831, the story by Charles Barrow in 1857, and the *Derby Mercury* column of 1883. The Revd Keith Osborn of the Peak Circuit of the Methodist Church, and Mrs Jennifer Fox, the circuit archivist, provided me with much-needed information about the history of Methodism in the area. Mrs Carol Longbone of the North Lincolnshire Libraries and Information Service located and photocopied the original account of the murder story in the *Arminian Magazine* for 1785. Kasia Drozdziak and colleagues in the Brotherton Special Collection at the University Library, Leeds, provided me with a copy of Jewitt's 1815 ballad based on the story. Peter Nockles and his colleagues at the John Rylands University Library, Manchester, gave me access to important rare volumes and to their (as yet incompletely indexed) collection of manuscripts relating to early Methodism. Beatrice Agutter of the National Archives of Scotland obtained copies for me of the *Derby Mercury* articles of 1829 and 1883 and carried out an exhaustive search for the alleged column in the *Caledonian Mercury* of 1819. The staff of the public libraries in Glossop, Buxton and Chapel-en-le-Frith, the Local Studies Libraries in Matlock and Derby, the Derbyshire Records Office and the Sheffield City Archives were unfailingly patient and cooperative with my quests for rare or obscure documents. I also benefited from discussions with Ruth Morgan, secretary of the Hunter Archaeological Society; Barbara Foster of the Derbyshire Archaeological Society; Fred and Mary Williamson of Dove Holes; Mithra Tonking, archivist of Lichfield Diocese; and Stuart Band, archivist of the Chatsworth Estate. Without the help and support of these people, I could not have completed more than a fraction of the necessary research.

Peter Harrison read the draft manuscript critically. His local knowledge was especially valuable in clarifying my thoughts about the historical basis of the story. Dr David Clarke (University of Sheffield) and Dr Caroline Oates (the Folklore Society's librarian) put me in touch with Dr Jacqueline Simpson of the Folklore Society, whose advice transformed my draft of the final chapter. She alerted me to a number of important publications that would otherwise have eluded me, and our prolonged correspondence opened my mind to a number of relevant aspects of folklore research. My sincere thanks are due to Jacqueline, and to the many others who enabled me to bring this project to a publishable state.

A summary version of this book has been published in the journal Folklore.

Mark P. Henderson

2010.

1

The Story in its Geographical and Cultural Setting

Britain underwent dramatic social and cultural changes during the eighteenth and early nineteenth centuries. New Christian denominations were founded. Overseas colonies were established. The Age of Reason (the Enlightenment) transformed intellectual life; it was succeeded by the era of Romanticism. Enclosures altered patterns of land ownership and access, enriching the few and impoverishing many. Factory-based industries led to an explosive growth of towns and cities, generating new wealth and terrible squalor. Transport and communications were revolutionised, first and foremost by the turnpike roads; and the earliest indications of tourism as a commercial enterprise were seen.

Access to the Peak District was difficult during the early eighteenth century, so it was partly insulated against some of these changes. But the insulation steadily yielded, and by the middle of the nineteenth century the region was no longer isolated. The metamorphosis of Britain was therefore mirrored in the Peak District, materially affecting the character and development of local life – and local folktales. It was during that period of transformation that the legend of the Winnats Pass murders arose.

This chapter portrays Castleton and its inhabitants as seen through the eyes of visitors to the area between the seventeenth and the early nineteenth centuries. Three aspects are emphasised because they are relevant to the ways in which the Winnats Pass murder story (WPM) evolved: the local lead mining industry, the beginnings of Methodism and the dawn of tourism. However, to provide a focus for what follows, here is a recent online variant of WPM, which contains most of the elements found in other modern variants[1]. As we shall see in chapters two-three, it is very different from earlier recorded accounts.

A Modern Variant of the Legend

Derbyshire's Own Gretna Green

Winnats Pass is a narrow limestone gorge which lies to the west of the village of Castleton and climbs a steady 1300 feet. Local legend has it that the Pass is haunted by the ghosts of two ill-fated lovers, murdered while they were on their way to be married at the 'runaway church' in the Peak Forest.

The Peak Forest chapel had been built in 1657 by Christiana, Countess of Devonshire. The chapel was 'extra parochial' and was exempt from the control of the ecclesiastical authorities. 'Foreign marriages' could be performed in this chapel which meant that couples from outside the parish could be wed there and as such marriages could go ahead without the normal legal requirement of banns being posted. The chapel became Derbyshire's own Gretna Green in a way and enabled couples who were perhaps facing objections to their marriage, to be legally wed.

This is exactly what Allan and Clara, a young couple from Scotland, were on their way to do in 1758.

A Premonition?

Allan's family were noble but poor and Clara's wealthy parents objected to the match to the point where Allan was threatened by Clara's brother. So the couple decided to elope to the Peak Forest chapel in Derbyshire. They had made their way to Stoney Middleton and stopped overnight in an inn there, the Royal Oak. During the night Clara had a terrifying dream in which she saw Allan being attacked and killed by robbers. She told Allan of the dream but they both put it down to the weariness of the journey.

They then made their way to Castleton and stopped for a rest and some refreshments at another inn before embarking on the final leg of their journey. A group of miners were also in the inn, quite raucous and drunk, and noticed that the couple were dressed in fine clothes. The miners overheard the landlord of the inn give directions to the couple to the chapel by way of Winnats Pass and once Allan and Clara had left they continued their drinking until a short time after when the landlord threw them out – presumably for drunkenness.

The group of men decided that by the look of the fine clothes of the couple it was likely that they would be carrying a substantial amount of money. They decided to rob them and so they set off to intercept the couple at Winnats Pass by taking a short cut stopping only to pick up another friend to come along with them.

Murder of the Young Lovers

As Allan and Clara were halfway through the Pass[2] the miners jumped out and dragged them from their horses. They found that the couple did indeed have some money – £200 – which they stole and after pushing the couple into a nearby barn they then had to decide what to do with them.

Allan realised that he and Clara were in danger and he pleaded for their lives but to no avail. Allan fought with the men only to be brutally beaten to death and Clara was then cruelly killed with the pickaxes that the miners had brought with them.

The men shared out the money between them and once it was dark they returned to the barn to dispose of the bodies.

Poetic Justice

The murder only came to light when one of the men on his death-bed confessed to the awful crime, probably to ease his conscience or in the fear of being refused entry into heaven. Whatever his reasoning he named the other men who had been involved but it seems that none of them ever benefited from the money that they stole and in one way or another fate seems to have punished all of them for their crime.

James Ashton, who had confessed on his death-bed, used his share of the ill-gotten gains to buy some horses but these all proved to be unfit animals and he died a poor man. Nicholas Cook and John Bradshaw both had accidents which killed them – Nicholas by falling from a buttress and John who was hit by a falling rock – coincidentally both these accidents happened close to the scene of the crime in Winnats Pass. Thomas Hall took his own life and hanged himself and Francis Butler, haunted by the memories of the crime, went insane.

Allan and Clara's horses were found on the fourth day after the murder and a saddle which is supposed to have been Clara's is on display in the museum at Speedwell Cavern.

Ten years later the bodies of Allan and Clara were discovered in a mineshaft. Sadly they never did make it to the 'runaway chapel' but their spirits are said to still wander Winnats Pass and sometimes can be heard begging for their lives.

Although the perpetrators of the crime were not punished in a legal sense, perhaps natural justice was done as they each suffered during their lifetime.

At this stage, it is worth noting three 'supernatural' elements in this story:

- The female victim ('Clara') had a premonition of the disaster – a precognitive dream.
- The murderers were punished not by human justice but by an invisible providence.
- The ghosts of the murdered couple now haunt the Winnats Pass.

We now turn to the location and the historical setting of these supposed events.

The Castleton Area

The Peak District of Derbyshire separates Manchester to the west from Sheffield to the east. Its northern extremity and its western and eastern fringes (the Dark Peak) are dominated by high moors with sandstone outcrops, its central and southern parts (the White Peak) by limestone

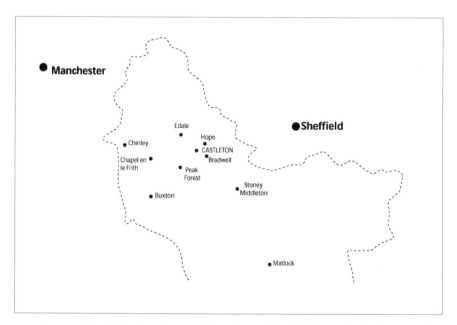

Sketch map of Peak District showing Manchester, Sheffield, Buxton, Castleton and Peak Forest.

hills and valleys. The Castleton area, which concerns us most directly, lies near the northern limit of the limestone region. It is picturesque and replete with interesting antiquities, but for most of the eighteenth century it was remote. It was also – to the surprise of many in the twenty-first century – industrial. These contrasts of beauty, remoteness, the relics of ancient history and the grim toil of lead mining and smelting constitute the background to the Winnats Pass murders.

Picturesque Beauty and Lead Mining

The Romantic idea of 'picturesque landscape' was an eighteenth century invention and became prominent in the nineteenth. However, the scenery of the Peak District acquired a reputation – albeit a mixed one – as early as the seventeenth century. William Camden specifically mentioned the castle and caves of Castleton in his pioneering Elizabethan guide-book of Britain, *Britannia* (Camden, 1610), but his judgment was lukewarm. Taylor (1618) was less than impressed by this part of England, and Michael Drayton railed against the ugliness of its wild hills in his interminably soporific alexandrines (Drayton, 1622):

> To th' unwearied Muse the Peake appears the while,
> A withered Beldam long, with bleared watrish eyes…
>
> Yee dark and hollow caves, the pourtraitures of Hell,
> Where Fogs and misty Damps continually doe dwell…

Edward Browne, writing in 1662, apparently described the area as 'strange' and 'wild' (Smith, 2004). In contrast, the long, ponderous poems of Hobbes (1668)[3] and Cotton (1683) were full of praise for the landscape. Among their 'seven wonders of the Peak', Hobbes and Cotton – like Drayton before them – included three features of the Castleton area: Eldon Hole ('Eldenhole') on Eldon Hill to the west of the village; Mam Tor, the 'shivering mountain' crowned with an Iron Age hill fort, to the north; and Peak Hole or Peak Cavern ('The Devil's Arse') on the western fringe of the village itself. These three features remain among the major attractions for the hordes of hikers, cavers and other tourists who visit the area every year and have done so ever since Hope station on the Manchester-Sheffield railway line was opened to passenger transport in 1894 (Tomlinson, 1985). (This railway line was enacted as early as 1831: DRO Q/RP/1/276/3-4.)[4]

However, the landscape of the White Peak, and the Castleton area in particular, has been sculpted not only by natural forces but also by centuries

The Castle of the Peak
('Peveril Castle').

The Peak Hole Water gorge
leading to the entrance to
Peak Cavern.

of agriculture and enclosures, and, crucially, by the long heritage of lead mining. The history and the peculiar customs, language and laws of that industry have been described in several publications, e.g. Ford and Rieuwerts (1968) and Rhodes (1973). Castleton was founded shortly after the Norman conquest as the garrison town for the Castle of the Peak ('Peveril Castle'), and by the thirteenth century it had a large market, which had faded almost to non-existence by the nineteenth century (Harrison, 2008)[5]; but it became a lead mining community and so it remained until well into the nineteenth century, when the British lead industry went into terminal decline.

In the late seventeenth century the intrepid traveller Celia Fiennes[6] wrote the following account of northern Derbyshire, where she visited each of the 'seven wonders' in turn (Morris, 1982):-

All Derbyshire is full of steep hills, and nothing but the peakes of hills as thick one by another is seen in most of the County which are very steepe which makes travelling tedious, and the miles long, you see neither hedge nor tree but only low drye stone walls round some grounds, else its only hills and dales as thick as you can imagine, but tho' the surface of the earth looks barren yet those hills are impregnated with rich Marbles Stones Metals Iron and Copper and Coale mines in their bowells, from whence we may see the wisdom and benignitye of our greate Creator to make up the deficiency of a place by an equivalent as also the diversity of the Creation which encreaseth its Beauty.

This passage highlights the difficulty of access to much of the Peak District at that time. Fiennes added the following remarks about the lead miners in the Castleton area:

... they dig down their mines like a well, for one man to be let down with a rope and pulley and so when they find the oar [sic], they keep digging under ground to follow the oar, which lies amongst the stone that lookes like our fire stones; in that mine I saw there was 3 or 4 at work and all let down thro' the well, they dig sometimes a great way before they come to oar; there is also a sort of stuff they dig out mixt with the oar and all about the hills they call it Sparr ... the doctors use it in medicine for the Collick ...

... they generally look very pale and yellow that work Underground, they are forc'd to keep lights with them and some times they are forced to use Gunpowder to break the stones, and that is sometimes hazardous to the people and destroys them at the work.

Ralph Thoresby (1677-1724), a Fellow of the Royal Society, visited Castleton on 20 July 1681 and his diary contains the following account of Mam Tor and the lead mining industry (Wright, 1831, pp. 7-9; Sheffield Archives Bag C/3363/11):

> The inhabitants positively affirm that it [Mam Tor] is neither larger nor less than in their infancy; notwithstanding there is, as I am now, and others in the company, have been many years eye witnesses of a continual flux of sand perpetually descending: so that it may well pass for the emblem of a liberal man never impoverished by his well bounded and grounded charity, his expenses being re-supplied by a secret Providence. From Castleton as I said having ascended the Peak, and riding some miles upon the mountains, there is digged up lead, the best in England, not to say Europe, and the best in quantity, improving yearly in the increase of it ...

A Lead Miner's Household in the Early Eighteenth Century

A generation after Thoresby and Fiennes, Daniel Defoe visited the Peak District during his tour through Great Britain. He was less favourably impressed by the landscape than Hobbes and Cotton, writing (Defoe 1724-6):

> Now to have so great a man as Mr Hobbes, and after him Mr Cotton, celebrate the trines here, the first in a fine Latin poem, the last in English verse, as if they were the most exalted wonders of the world: I cannot but, after wondering at their making wonders of them, desire you, my friend, to travel with me through this houling wilderness in your imagination, and you shall soon find all that is wonderful about it.

We might cavil at his judgment, as at Drayton's, but Defoe was a fine observer and reporter, and his humane account of the life and work of an early eighteenth-century lead miner is worth quoting *in extenso*. The events surrounding the Winnats Pass murders took place only a generation or two after Defoe wrote his travelogue, so we can presume that his descriptions of a miner's work and household were broadly applicable to the actors in that drama. A few paragraphs after the passage quoted above, he continued:

> The habitation was poor, 'tis true, but things within did not look so like misery as I expected. Every thing was clean and neat, tho' mean and

ordinary: There were shelves with earthen ware, and some pewter and brass. There was, which I observed in particular, a whole flitch or side of bacon hanging up in the chimney, and by it a good piece of another. There was a sow and pigs running about at the door, and a little lean cow feeding upon a green place just before the door, and the little enclosed piece of ground I mentioned, was growing with good barley; it being then near harvest.

To find out whence this appearance of substance came, I asked the poor woman, what trade her husband was? She said he worked in the lead mines. I asked her, how much he could earn a day there? She said, if he had good luck he could earn about five pence a day, but that he worked by the dish (which was a term of art I did not understand, but supposed, as I afterwards understood it was, by the great, in proportion to the oar, which they measure in a wooden bowl, which they call a dish)[7]. Then I asked, what she did? She said, when she was able to work she washed the oar ... But what can you get at washing the oar, said I, when you can work? She said, if she work'd hard she could gain three-pence a day. So that, in short, here was but eight-pence a day when they both worked hard, and that not always, and perhaps not often, and all this to maintain a man, his wife, and five small children, and yet they seemed to live very pleasantly, the children look'd plump and fat, ruddy and wholesome; and the woman was tall, well shap'd, clean, and (for the place) a very well looking, comely woman; nor was there any thing look'd like the dirt and nastiness of the miserable cottages of the poor; tho' many of them spend more money in strong drink than this poor woman had to maintain five children with ...

... [W]e went, by the direction of the poor woman, to a valley on the side of a rising hill, where there were several grooves, so they call the mouth of the shaft or pit by which they go down into a lead mine; and as we were standing still to look at one of them, admiring how small they were, and scarce believing a poor man that shew'd it us, when he told us, that they went down those narrow pits or holes to so great a depth in the earth; I say, while we were wondering, and scarce believing the fact, we were agreeably surprised with seeing a hand, and then an arm, and quickly after a head, thrust up out of the very groove we were looking at. It was the more surprising as not we only, but not the man that we were talking to, knew any thing of it, or expected it.

Immediately we rode closer up to the place, where we see the poor wretch working and heaving himself up gradually, as we thought, with difficulty; but when he shewed us that it was by setting his feet upon pieces of wood fixt cross the angles of the groove like a ladder, we found that the difficulty was not much; and if the groove had been larger they could not either go up or down so easily, or with so much safety, for that now their elbows resting on those pieces as well as their feet, they went up and down with great ease and safety ...

When this subterranean creature was come quite out, with all his furniture about him, we had as much variety to take us up as before, and our curiosity received full satisfaction without venturing down, as we were persuaded to by some people, and as two of our company were inclined to do.

First, the man was a most uncouth spectacle; he was cloathed all in leather, had a cap of the same without brims, some tools in a little basket which he drew up with him, not one of the names of which we could understand but by the help of an interpreter. Nor indeed could we understand any of the man's discourse so as to make out a whole sentence; and yet the man was pretty free of his tongue too.

For his person, he was lean as a skeleton, pale as a dead corps, his hair and beard a deep black, his flesh lank, and, as we thought, something of the colour of the lead itself, and being very tall and very lean he look'd, or we that saw him ascend *ab infernis*, fancied he look'd like an inhabitant of the dark regions below, and who was just ascended into the world of light.

Besides his basket of tools, he brought up with him about three quarters of a hundred weight of oar, which we wondered at, for the man had no small load to bring, considering the manner of his coming up; and this indeed made him come heaving and struggling up, as I said at first, as if he had great difficulty to get out; whereas it was indeed the weight that he brought with him ...

We asked him, how deep the mine lay which he came out of: He answered us in terms we did not understand; but our interpreter, as above, told us, it signified that he was at work 60 fathoms deep, but that there were five men of his party, who were, two of them, eleven fathoms, and the other three, fifteen fathoms deeper: He seemed to regret that he was not at work with those three; for that they had a deeper vein of oar than that which he worked in, and had a way out at the side of the hill, where they pass'd without coming up so high as he was obliged to do ...

We then look'd on the oar, and got the poor man's leave to bring every one a small piece of it away with us, for which we gave him two small pieces of better mettle, called shillings, which made his heart glad; and, as we understood by our interpreter, was more than he could gain at sixty fathoms under ground in three days; and we found soon after the money was so much, that it made him move off immediately towards the alehouse, to melt some of it into good Pale Derby; but, to his farther good luck, we were gotten to the same alehouse before him; where, when

A lead smelter. This engraving by Chantrey ('Smelting House in Middleton Dale') illustrates the type of construction that would have been common around Castleton and other lead mining centres in the eighteenth and early nineteenth centuries.

we saw him come, we gave him some liquor too, and made him keep his money, and promise us to carry it home to his family, which they told us lived hard by.

Castleton and the Oden Mine

Most lead miners drank heavily, believing that beer protected them against the toxic effects of the metal ore. They also smoked heavily, and their work was undoubtedly dangerous; but as Defoe observed, their families were healthy and well fed and the miners themselves were reputed to be 'long livers', though there were illnesses such as the smallpox outbreaks of 1753 and 1759 in Castleton, to say nothing of frequent accidents and suicides[8] (Shawcross, 1903; Rieuwerts, 1976). Defoe's account shows that mining families also kept livestock; generally, they were small-scale peasant farmers. Indeed, some workers in smaller and less productive mines divided their time between farming and the lead industry. For that reason, the land enclosures that followed the relevant Acts of 1691, 1781 and 1806 (DRO Q/RP/1/276/3-4) may have been socially divisive, effectively depriving many residents of their traditional access to common land. Those who had lost ancient grazing rights, and perhaps lands of their own, may have resented people – particularly outsiders – who were still obviously wealthy.

The economy of Castleton in the eighteenth century depended largely on mining and smelting of lead ore[9] (Rhodes, 1973), though the commercial value of lead fluctuated from decade to decade. Various subsidiary trades flourished: production of the leather clothes and hats[10] for miners, for example, and manufacture of tallow and wicks for candles (Harrison, 2008). Other essential members of the community included carriers to transport lead ore and coal to the smelters, and blacksmiths to make and repair mining tools and equipment. Although miners dominated the list of trades in the late eighteenth century, there were also weavers, tailors, husbandmen, bakers and curates (Shawcross, 1903). Rope makers, brewers and innkeepers were (for different though equally obvious reasons) indispensable in all mining communities, and Castleton had three different 'rope walks' and innumerable inns; apparently it also had a red light district (Harrison, 2008). There were eminent residents, too: the pioneering mineralogist Samuel Needham, 'the fossil man', whose was buried in St Edmund's churchyard; the mineralogist Mawe; and the geologist Elias Hall (Binney, 1860).

The immediate environs of Castleton were riddled with lead mines during the second half of the eighteenth century (Heathcote, 2007). The

Chantrey engraving of the 'Approach to Peaks Hole near Castleton' (compare the photograph on p. 16.). Peaks Hole was the location of the biggest of Castleton's three rope walks, places where ropes were made.

The cottages in modern-day Castleton were once the dwellings of lead miners. The photograph is taken from what used to be 'Treacle Street', the alleged red light district.

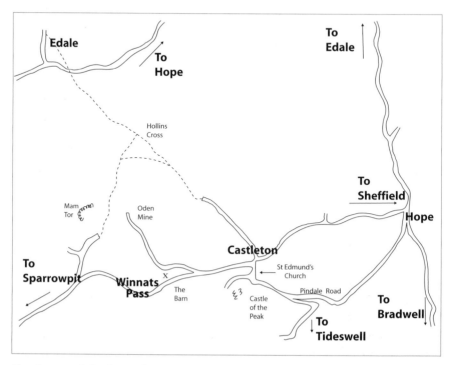

Sketch map of Castleton showing the Oden Mine, the Winnats Pass and the Pindale Road.

biggest and oldest of these, the Odin or Oden Mine[11], lay to the north-west of the village under the shadow of Mam Tor. It is traditionally held that at least some of the Winnats Pass murderers worked there[12]. The history, structure and productivity of the Oden has been described in summary and in full detail by leading authorities on local mining history (Rieuwerts, 1965, 1972, 1976; Ford and Rieuwerts, 1976). The mine was operational at or before 1280, and in the early eighteenth century its main vein – actually a series of nearly parallel veins connected by small scrins – proved very rich. In 1706, at least 41 men and 8 women were employed. Some miners earned up to 22/- (women 5/-) for a three-week stint. After 1726, large quantities of ore from the vein were mined in the Peak Forest Liberty, which adjoined the Castleton Liberty[13]. The Cartgate was opened in 1751-52, making it easier to move the ore from certain levels to the nearby crushing circle (Rieuwerts, 1976; Ford and Rieuwerts, 1976).

Like other Peak District villages, Castleton was an isolated community and its inhabitants were suspicious of and potentially hostile to outsiders, including those from neighbouring villages. This insularity and rivalry persisted even into the twentieth century and were evoked by Brooksbank (1925), who was Vicar of Castleton during the first decade of that century. The local dialect was largely incomprehensible to outsiders (Defoe, 1724-6; Brooksbank, 1925), and the community's inhabitants were mostly interrelated. That too remained a feature of Peak District villages for many years after the period of interest to us – witness this article in the *Derby and Chesterfield Reporter* (1832), cited by Flindall (2005):

> Persons visiting the scattered hamlets in the Peak, have often remarked that the inhabitants are mostly related to one another; the contented swains being seldom known to rove beyond the limits of the place of their nativity in search of the fair ones whose affections they seek to win. Perhaps this observation applies more particularly to those of Bradwell or Stoney Middleton ...

In such a community, wealthy strangers could have been perceived as fair game for robbers.

There were other industries besides lead mining, of which lime quarrying and burning were particularly important. West of Castleton, on the other side of the Winnats Pass, there was a lime kiln at Snitterton near the Eldon quarry (Harrison, 2008). Other kilns must also have been present in the area though their locations are not certain. The mining, cutting and polishing of the mineral blue john also became significant in the late eighteenth century[14].

View over Castleton and the Hope Valley to the hills that divide the Hope and Edale Valleys.

Accounts by Late Eighteenth Century Visitors

The Peak District, and not least the Castleton area, attracted increasing numbers of sightseers and travel writers in the late eighteenth century – the period when the WPM legend was beginning to circulate. This influx was partly due to the gradually improving system of roads, notably the Derby-Manchester turnpike that passed through Buxton (Dodd and Dodd, 2000; Bogart, 2004).

Pilkington (1789) began the first volume of his *View of the Present State of Derbyshire* with a panegyric on the view of the Hope-Castleton valley from the hill above the main (pre-turnpike) road to Sheffield.

Interestingly, Pilkington described Castleton as a town, while neighbouring Hope – not to mention Buxton, and also Matlock (now the county town) – were villages[15]. That suggests something about the relative size and commercial significance of Castleton during the heyday of lead mining[16]. However, Bray (1783) described Castleton as 'a small, poor town', an opinion confirmed by Harrison (2008), and Jewitt (1811) remarked of the hypothetical visitor to the area:

On entering the town his ideas change. He no longer remembers the plenty promised in the valley, nor sees cottages which appeared to him the abodes of contentment: he views nothing but a number of wretched huts, apparently inhabited by still more wretched inmates: he is every where assailed by clamours for his bounty, and is led to think as meanly of the town as but a few minutes before he thought highly of the vale in which it stands.

Pilkington was as interested in industry and commerce as he was in the picturesque, and his accounts of lead mining and smelting are minutely detailed[17]. Jewitt, however, was addressing the sightseer in search of the picturesque. This contrast reflects the transition from the Age of Reason to the era of Romanticism, though scientific interest in the land – both its mineralogy and its agriculture – was increasing at the same time (e.g. Nicholson, 1812; Farey, 1813).

Hutton (1816) visited Castleton at about the same time as Pilkington and, like Fiennes and Pilkington before him, was interested not only in the landscape and in the three 'wonders' listed by Hobbes and Cotton, but also in the lead mines and the miners. His autobiography contains a short account of that visit:

1785. Mounted the Castle-hill at Castleton; too steep for any attack. Examined the ruins, which seem to be Roman. The town below, and the adjacent views, were most charming. Penetrated to the extremity of Peak Hole, under the Castle-hill, more tremendous than pleasant. Ascended Mam Tor, or the Shivering Mountain, said continually to moulder, but not diminish, which is totally untrue, as may be seen by every observer. The mountain has diminished one-third in size, and a considerable hill has been raised from the detached parts. It kept mouldering all the time I was there, which I apprehend is chiefly owing to wet and thaw. This cannot amount in the least to a wonder, for every mountain will do the same which has a perpendicular side, composed of loose skerry-stones (and a light soil). Upon the summit is an extensive camp, not very secure (on one side). I returned by Elden Hole, a most terrific spectacle, a chasm lined with rock, thirty yards long and five wide, upon the declivity of a hill on Eldon Common, guarded by a wall. I threw down many stones, which produced five or six sounds in their descent, owing to the various bends in the passage, which is not perpendicular. I got among the mines and the miners; made inquiries, and paid money (for making them). They seemed a tarnished, ragged, and happy people. We should think the Peak inhabited by a race of beggars. I could not ask a question, or even inquire my road,

without 'Please, sir, to give me something.' I had a delightful walk (in
my return) over Peak Forest, but was affected at a village called Dam
(in the Forest)[18] at the sight of a number of people carrying to his house
a young man just killed in a mine. Arriving at Buxton in the evening, I
was much indisposed with liquors not accustomed to.

Hutton's experience of 'begging' by the local inhabitants seems similar to
Jewitt's.

A few years later, James Plumptre included an account of the Castleton
area in his tour of Britain (Ousby, 1992). Plumptre, like Pilkington and
Hutton, was equally fascinated by the picturesque and the practical, and –
again like Hutton – his descriptions juxtaposed the 'wonders' of Mam Tor,
Peak Hole and Eldon Hole with a visit to a lead mine and conversations
with the miners. He echoed Defoe in affirming that lead miners were
healthy people:

> It was four o'clock, the time the miners come from out the mine: the
> women, we observed, wore breeches. Here another Miner joined us,
> who was also to be the companion of our excursion. He was one of the
> stoutest men I ever saw: the very picture of health, well proportioned,
> and his muscles seemed of Herculean strength. It does not appear, from
> what we saw, that working in the mines is, as has been said, prejudicial
> to the health of either man or woman.

A young student, Carl Moritz, came to England from Berlin in 1782
specifically to see London, Oxford, and 'the wonders of the Peak Cavern
in Derbyshire' (Christian, 1996). The Castleton area was beginning to
achieve international fame.

Tourism

As the Romantic Movement gained momentum (Richards, 2002), tastes
among readers changed and 'wild nature' came to be celebrated while
industry was denigrated. Lord Byron famously wrote to a friend:

> Was you ever in Dovedale? I assure you there are things in Derbyshire as
> noble as in Greece or Switzerland.

But he made no mention of local industry and commerce.

By the second quarter of the nineteenth century, the Peak District had
become far more accessible thanks to of the network of turnpike roads

Sketch map showing the early turnpike roads from Derby to Manchester via Buxton, and from Manchester to Sheffield via Castleton.

that had by then penetrated much of the country (Dodd and Dodd, 2000; Bogart, 2004). Greater numbers of tourists were attracted because of the region's reputation for scenic beauty, and Buxton – which lay directly on a major turnpike – became a particular focus for them.

Buxton began its development into a popular spa town in the late eighteenth century, when the 5th Duke of Devonshire greatly improved its facilities by building the Crescent, which contained hotels, lodging houses and an Assembly Room. The Assembly Room, built in the early 1780s, was designed by the eminent architect John Carr of York. By 1789, the Great Stables were complete. Hall Bank was mainly built in the 1790s, the Square was completed in 1806, and the supply of town and lodging houses was further increased. Hutchinson (1809) was fulsome in his praise of the new buildings and described the alleged virtue of the waters in some detail, though Buxton was still considered a 'village' in 1820 and its facilities remained modest in comparison to those of Bath. There was a further series of improvements in the 1840s, and by the early 1850s Buxton had become a fashionable Victorian spa. Its population tripled each year during the season, when visitors flocked to it from all over the country, some to try the curative effects of the waters, some for rest and recreation, and others to enjoy the scenery and pastimes of the Peak District (Robertson, 1872; Langham and Wells, 1993).

The status of the Peak District as a picturesque tourist destination was foreshadowed in Jane Austen's *Pride and Prejudice* and in Anna Sewell's letters (Sewell, 1811) but was confirmed by the four-volume *Peak Scenery* by Rhodes[19] (1824), a popular success largely because of the superb illustrations by a local artist, Sir F. L. Chantrey, R.A. From the beginning of his book, Rhodes depicted the area as an oasis of rural peace between the grimy factory towns that bordered it on the east and west. Like Pilkington and Bentham he was entranced by the view over the Hope-Castleton valley:

> The Dale of Hope looked lovely from this commanding situation. A mild gleam of sunny light fell broad upon it, and for a while it was the only illuminated spot of ground within the wide horizon: the name of this sweet vale – the soft yet cheerful ray that now rested upon and lighted up its meadows, produced an association of pleasing images round which the mind lingered with delight.

But unlike Fiennes, Defoe, Pilkington and Plumpetre, he showed no interest in mining or miners, except (by implication) to associate them with the 'dark Satanic mills' that the Romantics of the early nineteenth century so fiercely – and understandably – deplored. That may be significant for the evolution of WPM. The Romantics idealised rural peasants but could readily have perceived lead miners as villains: mines and smelters were tantamount to factories; worse, they polluted the picturesque rural landscape. And the pioneering collectors of Peak District folklore such as Wood (1862) were typical exponents of Romanticism, particularly its Gothic facet.

Wood was also shrewd: he recognised the potential market for local tales among the summer tourists in Buxton, and as we shall see (chapter four), that was important in establishing the modern versions of WPM.

The Peak Forest Chapel

Rogerson (1901) gives a clear account of the peculiar status of the chapel in Peak Forest, the 'local Gretna Green', where the incumbent from 1747 to 1784 – the period of material interest for us – was John Ashe:

After the death of King Charles I. the Countess of Devonshire, a very loyal woman, and consequently much troubled at the execution of that monarch, sought some way of showing her loyalty and devotion. She decided on building a little church in the royal Forest, for the use of the King's Foresters. This she did in the year 1657 dedicating it to Charles King and Martyr ... The church built in the Royal Forest and on Crown land was under no jurisdiction, but had a Peculiar Jurisdiction of its own. It was also extra Parochial and extra Episcopal. The patronage has always been in the hands of the Devonshire family, and the Chapel was conveyed by deed of gift to the Minister. There was no institution or induction.

The Minister at Peak Forest had the right to hold a Peculiar Court and had the title of Principal Official and Judge in Spiritualities in the Peculiar Court of Peak Forest. In this court he granted Probate of Wills, &c. He had also power to grant Marriage Licences to any persons applying, no matter from whence they came, and in virtue of these Licences could marry any persons from anywhere and at any time. These powers he exercised in favour of people coming from all parts to this Ecclesiastical "Gretna Green" of the Peak. From ninety to a hundred of

The church of Charles, King and Martyr, in Peak Forest; it stands on the site of the old chapel.

these "Foreign Marriages," as they were locally called, took place every year. It is therefore very likely that many a tangled skein of family history may be unravelled by these Registers ... There remains an old document, date 1697, containing the answer of the minister to the Dane [sic] and Chapter of Lichfield. Among other matters he mentions the "records of more than threescore years", proof that there were records or registers for more than fifty years prior to those still in existence. After the year 1696 only a fragment remains until 1727... The Register of Foreign Marriages is a small folio, 16 inches by 8 inches, clearly written, and apparently only in two hands. In the latter part of it, the residences of the persons married are usually given.

Rogerson goes on to present information that – albeit tantalising – is potentially relevant to WPM (see chapter six). But whether his lucid account of the history and peculiar status of the chapel is also relevant to the story depends on whether the couple were indeed making for Peak Forest in order to marry, as most variants allege. He assumes that they were.

Here, however, the date of the incident becomes significant. The Hardwicke Act of 1754 had made it considerably more difficult for 'foreign marriages' to be celebrated in Peak Forest than they had previously been[20]. The Act became law in England and Wales but not in Scotland, which is why Gretna Green became the focus of runaway marriages after that date. Thus, if the traditional date of 1758 for the Winnats Pass murders is correct, the couple were probably not, after all, heading towards Peak Forest to be married. Conversely, if the couple's destination was indeed Peak Forest, the incident must have occurred before 1754.

Early Methodism in the Peak District

The earliest known written account of the Winnats Pass murders was composed by a pioneering Methodist preacher (see chapter two). The establishment of the new faith in the Peak District during the late eighteenth century therefore impinges on our investigation.

Methodism may be said to have originated in 1738, when John and Charles Wesley underwent a 'spiritual awakening', and to have become severed from the Church of England in 1784 when John Wesley first ordained ministers. The rise of Methodism was just one aspect of a surge in religious activity, the Evangelical Revival, that coincided with the Enlightenment (Ward, 1992; http://www.allsaintsjakarta.org/18centhist. htm). By 1749 there were some twenty Methodist circuits in England;

one, the Sheffield circuit, encompassed the Peak District[21], while Buxton alternated between the Macclesfield and Leek circuits (Leach, 1985). John Wesley himself preached at the Towngate in Bradwell in 1747 while on his way from Chinley to Sheffield (Evans, 1907; Ogle, 1998); Chinley was home to John Bennet, an early preacher who had become associated with Wesley in 1743 (Leach, 1985).

Bradwell was much more receptive to the Puritan-derived teachings of Methodism than many villages in the area. That was partly because of its remarkable Nonconformist tradition; Bradwell's Presbyterian Chapel had been built in the 1660s for the 'Apostle of the Peak', William Bagshawe of Chapel-en-le-Frith (1628-1702), who was ejected from the vicarage of Glossop for nonconformity[22] (Bagshawe, 1887). Also, there was a strong spirit of independence in the village – many of the lead miners were self-employed and most owned their own homes – and that too may have encouraged the people to embrace a new faith that fostered independence and dissent from established authority. William Allwood, a minister from Rotherham, preached in the village in 1750 and induced a number of conversions. One outstanding Bradwell resident, the mining agent Benjamin Barber, became the mainstay of the cause and was instrumental in converting many of the local miners (Evans, 1907). Methodism became a considerable civilising influence on Bradwell and subsequently on other Peak District villages.

Many of the earliest Methodist services were held in barns and other farm buildings, often quite remote from the villages. Indeed, Wesley himself preached in the barn where all the early meetings in Bradwell took place. Benjamin Barber caused the first Methodist Chapel to be built in the village in 1768. Chapels were subsequently built at Grindleford Bridge in 1776, Sparrowpit around 1790, Eyam in 1793 and Baslow in 1796 (Ogle, 1998), indicating the speed with which the faith spread through the Peak District during the late eighteenth century. Its dissemination was often peaceful, though not always. Hooligans sought to cause trouble when Matthew Mayer of Stockport first preached in Eyam, in 1765, but Mayer's oration was so impressive that the disruption was stillborn. Hathersage was less fortunate; a preacher was driven out of that village 'through violence of persecution' (Ogle, 1998). The pioneering minister John Nelson of Birstall, Yorkshire, was attacked by the local clergyman and a gang of drunken lead miners when he preached in Monyash in 1750 (Leach, 1985).

One of the earliest ministers of the new faith, David Taylor, was a butler from Heeley, Sheffield. He brought Methodism to the Sparrowpit area during the late 1740s. In 1750, he was caught at night in a blizzard in the Edale valley and sought shelter at a lonely farmhouse. On hearing the knock at the door, the farmer, Joseph Hadfield, reached for his sword; he had fought as a soldier during the Jacobite rising five years earlier and knew there were Jacobite refugees in the area. But David Taylor called 'Peace be to this house' and was admitted. Before the night was over, Joseph Hadfield was a convert (Ogle, 1998) and Methodism was introduced peacefully into Edale. One Edale resident who was subsequently converted, the tax collector Thomas Marshall, played a crucial part in establishing the WPM legend (chapter two). However, the introduction of the new faith to Castleton was considerably less pacific.

Benjamin Barber of Bradwell accepted an invitation to preach in Castleton, along with a visiting minister, in the early 1760s. Several residents assembled for the occasion, but an antagonistic mob gathered outside, led by three servants of the village squire, beating old kettles and pans and a drum. Their attempt to disrupt the service failed. When the two preachers subsequently went to Mrs Slack's house for supper, the mob burst in, but Mrs Slack drove a knife through the drumskin, putting an end to the music. The assailants then climbed on to the roof and dropped cows' entrails down the chimney. The preachers waited a while for the rabble to disperse before they departed, but their ill-wishers ambushed them on the road to Bradwell and pelted them with missiles, to their considerable injury. The incident[23] was typical of the way in which pioneering Methodist preachers were received in many parts of Britain, though it probably also reflected the long-term rivalry between Castleton and Bradwell (Brooksbank, 1925).

Two days later, a ringleader of the mob was ordered to reconcile one of the squire's young horses to the use of firearms, so he went to the stable with a loaded pistol in his pocket. The pistol accidentally discharged and killed him. The Methodists were quick to deem this fatality an act of Divine judgement, and their preachers were never again exposed to excessive shows of brute force in that part of the world. The possible relevance of the incident to WPM will become apparent in the following chapter.

The Winnats Pass Murders as History

It is generally (though not universally) agreed that a group of local men did indeed rob and murder a wealthy couple at the entrance to the Winnats Pass in the mid-eighteenth century, and that variants of the legend recount the incident more or less fancifully. No civilised society condones robbery or murder, but we should consider the crime from the standpoint of the perpetrators and their community. Notwithstanding Defoe's remarks, they were poor people who lived hard, dangerous lives. Their lot was worsened by an increasing tax burden – not least on horses and on beer (Olsen, 1999)[24] – and by the loss of common land through enclosures (Bogart, 2004). Inevitably, therefore, closed working communities such as Castleton not only envied the rich but also blamed them for their own privations. Local robbers could therefore expect a considerable degree of sympathy and protection from their neighbours and kin, at least when the victims were unknown outsiders who were travelling through their territory. But why murder?

Punishments were extreme in eighteenth century England; robbers, like murderers, faced hanging if they were convicted. Therefore, by killing their victims after robbing them, the perpetrators courted no more serious punishment; on the contrary, they were much less likely to be detected and prosecuted, provided they hid the bodies. There was no police force, and although entrepreneurial thief-takers (bounty hunters, in effect) had been in operation since the early part of the century (Olsen, 1999), they would not have ventured into a Peak District mining community, and would have enjoyed no success (and certainly no welcome) had they done so.

In general, thieves were prosecuted privately in eighteenth century England, usually by their victims (Friedman, 1995). They could escape the gallows by two means: compensating the victim, or arranging for a person of high status to plead for their pardon.

Strictly speaking, compensation arrangements ('compounding') between criminal and victim were legal only for minor misdemeanours, not major felonies, but that applied only if the criminal had been formally charged. If the perpetrator agreed to pay an acceptable recompense, the victim would withdraw the prosecution or threat of prosecution: no charge, no court appearance.

The alternative – arranging a plea for pardon – would have entailed a *quid pro quo*. The local squire or vicar might agree to intervene in exchange for useful services by the criminal. The squire or vicar might then ask a local member of parliament or peer (in exchange, say, for support at the next election) to assure the court that the criminal was actually a person of good character and should be pardoned, or at worst transported rather than hanged.

Friedman (1995) estimates that because of these devices, only about 16 per cent of people arrested for capital offences in the eighteenth century actually went to the gallows.

Had they been apprehended, the Winnats Pass murderers would almost certainly have figured among Friedman's 16 per cent. Suppose they had released their victims after the robbery, and the victims had demanded recompense as the alternative to prosecution. What could poor lead miners have offered that would have been acceptable to such wealthy travellers?

As for the alternative, it is unlikely that they could have offered services that would have persuaded local gentry to plead for them, and it is far from clear that the gentry could have prevailed upon a local MP or peer[25] to intervene with the court. If the perpetrators of the crime were aware of these considerations, as we should assume, then they acted *rationally* by murdering and burying their victims after the robbery.

In short: from their point of view, as for most eighteenth-century footpads, the robbery was justifiable and the subsequent murder was a sensible course of action. In areas such as the Peak District, the strict moral code of Methodism provided one of the few effective counters to such reasoning prior to the development of police forces and public prosecutions in the nineteenth century.

2

The Earliest Written Account

We shall leave the historical basis of the story in the background until chapter six and focus on the legend itself. The first published version (Hanby, 1785) appeared in the *Arminian Magazine*, the periodical of the young Methodist church[1]. Here it is in full:

The following melancholy Account was given me by a very worthy man, Mr *Thomas Marshall* of *Edal* in Derbyshire, Dec. 17, 1778.

Twenty years ago, a young Gentleman and Lady came out of Scotland, as is supposed, upon a matrimonial affair. As they were travelling through that county, they were robbed and murdered, at a place called the Winnets, near Castleton. Their bones were found about ten years ago, by some miners who were sinking an Engine-pit at the place.

One James Ashton of Castleton, who died about a fortnight ago, and who was one of the murderers, was most miserably afflicted and tormented in his conscience. He had been dying, it was thought, for ten weeks; but could not die till he had confessed the whole affair. But when he had done this, he died immediately.

He said, Nicholas Cock, Thomas Hall, John Bradshaw, Francis Butler, and himself, meeting the above Gentleman and Lady in the Winnets, pulled them off their horses, and dragged them into a barn belonging to one of them, and took from them two hundred pounds. Then seizing upon the young Gentleman, the young Lady (whom Ashton said was the fairest woman he ever saw) intreated them, in the most pitious manner, not to kill him, as she was the cause of his coming into that country. But, notwithstanding all her intreaties, they cut his throat from ear to ear! They then seized the young Lady herself, and though she intreated them, on her knees, to spare her life, and turn her out naked! yet one of the wretches drove a Miner's pick into her head, when she dropt down dead at his feet. Having thus dispatched them both, they left their bodies in the barn, and went away with their booty.

At night they returned to the barn, in order to take them away; but they were so terrified with a frightful noise, that they durst not move them; and so it was the second night. But the third night, Ashton said, it was only the Devil, who would not hurt him; so they took the bodies away, and buried them.

They then divided the money: and as Ashton was a Coal-Carrier to a Smelt-Mill, on the Sheffield Road, he bought horses with his share; but they all died in a little time. Nicholas Cock fell from a precipice, near the place where they had committed the murder, and was killed. Thomas Hall hanged himself. John Bradshaw was walking near the place where they had buried the bodies, when a stone fell from the hill and killed him on the spot, to the astonishment of every one who knew it. Francis Butler, attempted many times to hang himself, but was prevented; however he went mad, and died in a most miserable manner.

Thus, though they escaped the hand of human justice (which seldom happens in such a case) yet the hand of God found them out, even in this world. How true then is it, that thou, O Lord, art about our path, and about our bed, and spiest all our ways!
THOMAS HANBY

What were this preacher's motives for telling such a story in his denomination's official magazine, and what impact would it have had on his readers?

The Author of the Article

Harmon (1974) and Lewis (1995) give brief outlines of the life and ministry of Thomas Hanby (1733-96). A chapter in Jackson (2002) provides more detail, comprising an autobiographical letter to John Wesley sent from Liverpool on 12 November 1779, and obituaries by his Methodist friends T. Bartholomew and J. Pawson, written shortly after his death in Nottingham on 29 December 1796. Some details, mainly derived from Jackson (2002), are given on several websites (see footnotes to the following paragraphs). The rest of the information in this section was obtained from Hanby's letters (John Rylands Library PLP 48.55). His long and successful circuit ministry has been described as follows[2]:

A pillar in the house of God, he manfully bore the "burden and heat of the day," meekly endured severe persecution, and cheerfully submitted to the painful privations to which the early Methodist Preachers were unavoidably subjected. The genuineness of his piety and the amiability of his disposition were only equalled by his firm and unflinching regard for the truth. He was an acceptable and useful minister, and was universally beloved by the people.

Hanby was born in Carlisle, the youngest of three children of a woollen factory manager. Orphaned when he was seven, he was brought up by his aunt in Barnard Castle and raised as an Anglican; the dissolute lives of his father and uncle clearly left a mark on him. He did not distinguish himself at school and was put out to a trade when he was twelve, becoming a stuff-maker.

His conversion to Methodism was gradual, but a shoemaker called Joseph Cheesborough was instrumental in it. Cheesborough worked in Leeds but had returned to his native Barnard Castle; he did not 'preach or exhort ... but imparted truth by friendly discourse with former acquaintances'. Thanks mainly to Cheesborough's influence, Hanby attended Methodist services – initially it seems in the company of other youths intent on disrupting proceedings, but later with genuine interest. He grew familiar with the violence visited on the early preachers:

> After Mr Whitford, we were favoured with Mr Tucker, Mr Turnough, Mr John Fenwick, Mr Rowel, and others; who often preached to us while the blood ran down their faces, by the blows and pointed arrows thrown at them while they were preaching.

Travelling first to Newcastle, then to Leeds, he found himself drawn to the idea of preaching but suffered agony of mind about the prospect. He was finally persuaded by a good woman on her death-bed, who assured him that God had called him. He entered the itinerancy in 1754 at the age of 21, becoming the first Methodist preacher in Ashbourne[3]. He met violent opposition when he preached in the high street there[4]:

> In 1754 Brother Mitchell desired me to come and help them in the Staffordshire Circuit for a few months. I made an excursion into the wilds of Derbyshire, preached at Wootton, near Weaver Hill, the Ford, Snelson, and Ashbourne, where there had been no such a being as a Methodist preacher ...
>
> I left Ashbourne for about a fortnight, to visit my new friends in Snelson etc. – and returned again. I now found I must preach no more

at the toll-gate house: the commissioners of the road had forbidden my friend, Mr Thompson to admit me. But Mr Hurd, a gentleman farmer, by the desire of his family, whose hearts God had touched, suffered me to preach at his house. It was now that a furious mob arose while I was preaching, and beset the house, and sprang in among us like so many lions. I soon perceived that I was the object of their rage. My mind was variously agitated, yet I durst not but cry aloud as long as I could be heard; but at last I was overpowered with noise. Some of my friends, in defending me, were bleeding among the mob, and with difficulty I escaped out of their hands. But as Mr Thompson, Mr Isaac Peach, Mr Hurd's family, Miss Beresford and a few others remained steady, I was constrained to repeat my visits, till the Lord gave us peace.

His phrase 'the wilds of Derbyshire' is notable, once again emphasising the remoteness of the Peak District in the mid-eighteenth century; though at the time of the alleged Winnats Pass murders (and certainly when the legend was starting to spread), the growing network of turnpike roads had begun to improve access, as we have seen. Hanby's experience of mob violence was not confined to Ashbourne. He faced similar opposition in Leek and was almost killed in Ashby-de-la-Zouche, and again in Burton:

In weariness and painfulness, in hunger and thirst, in joy and sorrow, in weakness and trembling, were my days now spent.

Clearly, he was a man of strong faith and considerable courage and determination. In 1755, he was sent to Canterbury, where he was robbed of all his money and valuables by two footpads. He described his subsequent sojourn in Scotland, particularly Dundee in 1763, as the happiest period of his life. On the 4 of June 1757 he had married Hannah Allen; but she died, along with their only child, in 1765. He later re-married and his second wife, Jenny, gave birth to twin daughters in on 13 November 1789.

His life as an itinerant preacher took him over much of mainland Britain. His circuit appointments after he left Dundee were: Leeds 1765, Birstall 1766, Staffordshire 1767, Bedfordshire 1768, Newcastle 1769-70, Edinburgh and Glasgow 1771-2, Staffordshire 1772-3, Gloucestershire 1774-5, Macclesfield 1776-7, Liverpool 1778-81, Staffordshire 1781, Birmingham 1782, Burslem 1783, Dundee 1785-6[5], Sheffield 1787, Nottingham 1788, Bolton 1789-90, Oldham 1791-2, Leeds 1793-4 and Nottingham 1795-6. He was appointed a member of the Legal Hundred in 1784. In 1794, he was chosen President of the Conference in Bristol. He died two years later, having long suffered from gallstones.

Portrait of Thomas Hanby.

Notwithstanding the great respect in which he was held by most of his fellow-ministers and his congregations (for example, Thomas Coke's letters to him reveal warm friendship: John Rylands Library PLP 28.6/10-12), he had fallen into dispute with John Wesley and others about the administration of the Sacraments (Lewis, 1995). Writing to his friend the Revd Mr Bogie of Berwick-upon Tweed on 27 February 1789, he expressed his resolution in this matter:

> Believe me, I act not from Wrath, but Conscience. I expect Mr Wesley and Mather will shew me no mercy, you know I am obnoxious to the latter, and in no very great esteem with the former. However I have the testimony of my Conscience that I only meen [sic] to do the will of God, and he has made me willing to suffer it.

Writing to the same correspondent on 5 August that same year, he suggested that the problem had been resolved and that he was then on his way to Leeds; but the issue still seemed to rankle as late as 1794 (John Rylands Library PLP 48.55/11, 19, 22).

So why did this pioneering Methodist preacher, at the age of fifty-one, while he was involved in a doctrinal dispute with the founder of the young denomination, choose to write an account of the Winnats Pass murders in the *Arminian Magazine*?

The Beginnings of a Legend

Despite their disagreement about the Sacraments, Hanby and Wesley were of the same mind in other matters, not least the reality and significance of supernatural agencies (Ward, 1992; Davies, 2002). Davies (2002) wrote in the abstract of his article:

> During the second half of the eighteenth century and the early nineteenth century, there was growing concern that the popular belief in witchcraft and magic was still widespread ... During the same period, the growing popularity of Methodism was also worrying the Anglican establishment. With the likes of John Wesley openly expressing their belief in witchcraft, possession, and divine intervention and retribution, it was not surprising, perhaps, that Anglicans sought to blame Methodism for the continued, pernicious 'superstitious' state of the masses.

The compilation of letters, anecdotes, reflections and scriptural commentaries by Tregortha (1806)[6] illustrates the significance of supernatural agencies for Methodists at that time. Tregortha's preface contains the summary statement (p. vii):

> The reality therefore of the apparitions of angels, daemons, and departed souls, cannot be denied, without destroying the authority of the scriptures, which relate and suppose them.

In that sense, Hanby's *Arminian Magazine* article would have assured readers of his doctrinal correctness: the story emphasised the vengeful power of God in the everyday world, according fully with early Methodist teaching. It illustrates the principle that the ungodly: 'shall not live out half their days ... the wicked is driven away in his wickedness'[7]. The story may have had personal significance for Hanby as well: the alleged murderers were his contemporaries, and they were all dead while he was still living; and he himself had suffered an attack from footpads (see above).

There seems little doubt that he saw a ready-made homily or sermon in the Winnats Pass murders. In order to drive home this moral point, he had to make the sorry fates of the five alleged murderers into the focus of his article. That showed Divine retribution in action: the first of the three 'supernatural' elements in the tale as we have it today. The 'terrible noise' that allegedly frightened the murderers when they returned to the barn on the night of the crime serves to dramatise that element. Moreover, Ashton's implicit salvation through confession (he died with his conscience presumably cleared by admission of guilt) is a further feature of the traditional Christian – including Methodist – message. Hanby's motive for recounting the story is therefore clear: he was giving a sermon. His compressed, plain, unadorned prose is characteristic of early Methodist sermons and typifies Puritan distaste for ornament and elaboration. He was not content merely to preach to the converted, in this case to fellow-readers of the *Arminian Magazine*. Like all his colleagues he was an indefatigable proselytiser. Hence, presumably, his almost word-for-word copy of the *Arminian* article in the more widely-read *Derby Mercury* in the same month (April 1785); see Appendix I. The version published in Tregortha (1806, pp. 247-249) is also virtually identical except that the name 'Cock' has become 'Cook'. John Tregortha had almost certainly read the story in the *Arminian Magazine,* but since he lived in Burslem, he is also likely to have met its author while Hanby was in that town in 1783-84; so he may have heard a version of it before it was published. The several editions of Tregortha's book ensured that the tale was widely read and it doubtless became a favourite topic of Methodist sermons, not least in the Peak District.

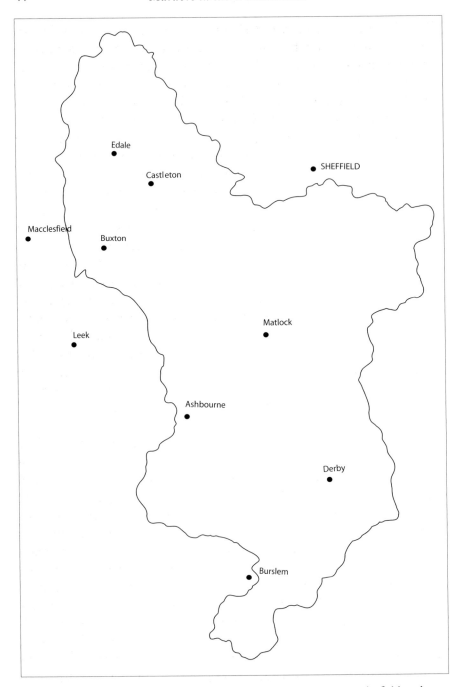

Sketch map of Derbyshire showing Ashbourne, Burslem, Leek, Macclesfield and Sheffield – towns in which Hanby worked – and also Castleton and Edale.

The circumstances under which Hanby first learned the story from Thomas Marshall (and/or his wife: Appendix I) are not clear. Marshall gathered duties on horses from the whole of Derbyshire and part of Staffordshire (Derby Local Studies Library MS 9237 052 No. 106) and he was certainly a Methodist[8], possibly related to Elias Marshall of Bradwell (the founder of 'Marshall's Charity'), probably converted to the faith along with many other Edale residents after 1750 (see chapter one). He was probably a generation younger than Hanby; he is recorded as marrying Betty Senior in 1774 (DRO D1432 A/P1/1/1-2). Hanby had moved to Liverpool in 1778, but he may still have visited or passed through Derbyshire that December – or Marshall may have visited Liverpool on business. They probably had Methodist acquaintances in common. In any case, since both men travelled quite widely, they may have met on more than one occasion.

Why did Hanby wait more than six years after hearing the story before he published it in the *Arminian Magazine*? His decision to make it public in 1785 may have been a defensive response to John Wesley's reprimand about the Sacraments, as suggested earlier. We know from his own account (Jackson, 2004) that his sojourn in Scotland around 1760 had been the 'happiest period of his life', so he must have been eager to return to that country. Wesley planned to send three ministers to Scotland to reinforce Methodism there in 1785. By publishing his sermon based on the Winnats Pass murders in April of that year, Hanby probably helped to ensure his place among the three.

Were he alive today, he would no doubt regret that the story has evolved into a folktale shorn of his moral and religious message. Ironically, his main device for illustrating that message – emphasising the series of disasters that befell the killers – may be primarily responsible for the tale's enduring popularity. The hand of fate falling upon evil-doers is a universal theme, common among novels, plays, films, children's stories and especially folktales, and this 'supernatural' element has survived in almost every variant of WPM up to the present time. Had the first written version not been dominated by that element, the tale may not have survived at all. The brief *Arminian Magazine* account describes an ugly but commonplace crime, scarcely the subject for a durable story, and it contains no details about the victims that could excite our sympathy or interest. The murdered lady and gentleman serve only to provide an occasion for that wickedness of which the perpetrators would subsequently be punished by God – or, perhaps, redeemed by virtue of repentance. But as we shall see, Hanby deployed rhetorical tricks that must have impressed a late eighteenth century audience, making the story powerful – not least to residents of the Castleton area who heard it. His version would probably have fused with orally-circulating forms of the story in the neighbourhood, markedly increasing its appeal and therefore its chances of survival, notably among the poorer classes to whom the Methodists particularly directed their attention.

Analysis

These points established, we can now examine the *Arminian Magazine* story in more detail. It is obviously tendentious, as already discussed, but a man of Hanby's character is unlikely to have invented or repeated a story in which real people, whose families still lived in Castleton or the surrounding area, were gratuitously portrayed as evil-doers. We therefore infer that Hanby believed the tale. Nevertheless, the following observations cast doubt on its accuracy.

- It is often supposed (e.g. Eisenberg, 1992) that James Ashton made his death-bed confession to the Vicar of Castleton, who in 1778 was the Revd Francis Herbert Hume[9]. But a death-bed confession to a clergyman is not to be made public, not even to be shared with a 'worthy man' such as Thomas Marshall of Edale (Edal). Suppose, instead, that Ashton told the story directly to Marshall; perhaps Marshall and his wife were attending the sick man. We would then have: (a) Hanby's tendentious retelling of (b) Marshall's recollection of (c) a mortally ill man's supposed reminiscence of an event that had taken place 'twenty years earlier'. A court of law would not consider such evidence admissible. Yet this scenario – which makes Hanby's story third-hand – assumes the most direct chain of communication possible. Marshall may have heard the story indirectly rather than from Ashton himself, in which case Hanby's account was at best fourth-hand.
- The implications are evident: at least three of the 'facts' reported by Hanby are distorted. First, if Marshall told the story to him in mid-December 1778, then Ashton had died two months earlier, not a fortnight earlier; his burial is recorded as 18 October, 1778 (DRO D1432 A/P1/1/1-2). Second, although Nicholas Cock indeed died in a fall from a precipice (he was buried on 29 December, 1766, the day after the inquest into his death), the accident occurred at Blackwell, some seven miles south of Castleton (Flindall, 2005), not 'near the place where they had committed the murder'. Third, although the story that Ashton was a coal-carrier has persisted (and indeed there was a smelt-mill – a cupola furnace – on the old Sheffield road, i.e. the Pindale road), he was actually recorded as a carter working at the Oden Mine during the 1750s (Rieuwerts, 1976). These are minor discrepancies, but they

cast some doubt on the remainder of Hanby's story. Without impugning Hanby's integrity, therefore, we have to regard the historical accuracy of the *Arminian Magazine* article with some scepticism.

- The account does not state that the couple were on their way to Peak Forest to be married (though it may imply that they were). That destination is assumed as fact in most variants of WPM, but there is no reliable supporting evidence.

- The 'twenty years' that are supposed to have elapsed between the date of the crime and Ashton's confession must be considered approximate at best. Even people in good health and of sound mind would find it hard to estimate such a lapse of time by memory; and Ashton on his death bed was in far from good physical (or presumably mental) health. There is no firm independent evidence to support the 1758 date, so we may challenge it.

- Both the gentleman and the lady are supposed to have 'come out of Scotland'. That might only mean that they were not local. After the troubles of 1745, Jacobite refugees were familiar and probably disturbing arrivals in the Castleton area, where outsiders were otherwise a rarity. That might have led to the presumption that any 'foreigner' was 'Scottish'[10]. Also, there was a general tendency among Peak District villagers to describe travelling people such as peddlers as 'Scotsmen'. But whatever their origins, why were the couple travelling through the Winnats Pass? It was certainly an odd route to the Peak Forest chapel. We shall consider that question in chapter six.

- If 'their bones were found about ten years ago' (which might mean about 1768 or about 1775), why is there no record of any inquest on the remains, or of their being reburied in consecrated ground (Flindall, 2005)? That question might be answerable (see chapter six), but it points to a difficulty with the story.

- Where was the 'Engine-pit' being sunk, leading to the discovery of the victims' remains? On the face of it, the likeliest guess seems the Speedwell Mine, very close to the barn at the foot of the Winnats Pass. The dates would fit: Thomas Bennet bought the rights to New Rake, the southernmost vein of lead ore in Speedwell, in 1771, and mining probably began there in 1774[11]. However, the land around the shaft is very rocky and therefore unsuitable for the hasty burial of bodies. An alternative site may be the other side of the road, where the Speedwell Cavern shop now stands; the depth of soil would have been greater there. There was also a good depth of soil near the barn itself. But neither of these possible sites was ever the location of an engine-shaft. This question remains unresolved.

- The barn 'belonged to one of the murderers'. It is curious that Hanby (or his informant) was not more specific. Which of the murderers

A view over the remains of the Speedwell Mine at the foot of the Winnats Pass, looking north-eastwards across the Hope Valley.

owned the barn? It is also curious that few subsequent variants of WPM have mentioned this detail. The question will be pursued in chapter six.

- The gentleman seems to have been surprisingly passive in this version of the story (unlike many later variants). He said nothing and did nothing. The lady's role was considerably more active. Perhaps the gentleman was overpowered and immobilised before his throat was 'cut from ear to ear', and his comments on the occasion did not bear repetition by a Methodist preacher. Otherwise, his passivity seems inconsistent with his role as guardian of a lady, especially one he apparently intended to marry. However, it is typical of European folktales that only one participant in the story is active, or speaks, at any one time, and that dialogues involve no more than two persons (Olrik, 1965). So this apparently strange feature of Hanby's account may indicate that the legend of the Winnats Pass murders was already a folktale – already in oral circulation – when Thomas Marshall apprised him of it.
- If so, then it was already in circulation before Ashton's confession, which was made only a few weeks before Marshall apparently told the story to Hanby.

- The lady declared of the gentleman that 'she was the cause of his coming into that country'. Could that suggest that she lived somewhere near Castleton, and that her companion had collected her from home, perhaps to marry her at Peak Forest – or for some other purpose?
- The lady further asked the murderers to 'turn her out naked'. Removing the victims' clothes was common practice among footpads, partly because the clothes of wealthy people were valuable, and partly because the absence of clothes would make the bodies more difficult to identify; there was no such thing as 'forensic evidence' in the mid-eighteenth century. And it is much easier to remove people's clothes while they were alive than when they are dead.
- No mention is made of the couple's horses, another element that features in later variants of the tale. The horses of a wealthy couple must have been valuable but the robbers did not take them, possibly because any attempt to divide two horses among five men could have led to disputes. In any case, had any of them suddenly acquired an expensive horse, their risk of detection would have been greatly increased.
- The murderers were obliged to return to the barn on three successive nights before they succeeded in burying the bodies. That again suggests a folktale: the threefold repetition of an event, the third instance differing from the first two, is a well-established feature of European folklore[12] (Olrik, 1965).

The Rhetorical Force of the Story

More than two centuries have elapsed since Hanby's account was written, making it difficult to evaluate in the context of its time. However, in the light of what we know about early Methodism in the Peak District, several rhetorical features stand out. One, already discussed, is the emphasis on Divine retribution – the invisible but implacable hand of Providence. The other features are less immediately obvious.

There is a striking parallel between Hanby's story and the first introduction of Methodism to Castleton (Evans, 1907; Ogle, 1998), described in chapter one. It is a matter of historical fact that when they first preached the new faith in the village, Benjamin Barber and his colleague were accosted by a mob of local ill-wishers. The victims were injured, apparently almost fatally in Barber's case. Soon afterwards, a ringleader of the mob was killed in a curious accident and the fatality was attributed to Divine retribution. In Hanby's account of the Winnats Pass murders, strangers visiting Castleton (the lady and gentleman 'from Scotland') were accosted by a mob from the village. They were robbed and killed. Soon afterwards, most of the assailants died violently, and Divine retribution was again inferred. Anyone in the area who read Hanby's account – or heard a sermon based on it – could not have failed to see the parallel. It would have lent considerable force and immediacy to the moral message.

The female victim's supplication to the murderers stands in contrast to the male's passivity. By making the killers ignore the woman's plea, Hanby emphasises their mercilessness. In the minds of his readers (or congregation), such cruelty to a defenceless woman would have merited no amelioration of Divine Justice.

As we have seen, Methodists were often obliged to hold their services either out of doors or, commonly, in barns belonging to those who sympathised with the cause; a barn in Bradwell was used regularly for that purpose for several years. It was therefore viciously ironic to have made a barn 'belonging to one of the murderers' the scene of the Winnats Pass atrocity. To Hanby's readers or listeners, that detail could have portrayed the murders as an evil parody of a Methodist service, further enhancing the force of his message.

For these and perhaps other reasons, this version of the legend became strongly established. In addition to the copy in Tregortha (1806), it was repeated – essentially unaltered – in the Wolley manuscript and in three *Derby Mercury* articles spanning the next 100 years (Appendix I). Although those variants show little evolutionary development, they helped to keep Hanby's version in the public eye.

However, some of the many versions of WPM written during the following century were at least partially independent of Hanby's influence. They will be the subject of the next chapter.

Ancient and Modern Variants

It is interesting to compare and contrast the modern online variant quoted at the beginning of chapter one with Hanby's original version. Most of the elements[13] of Hanby (1785) are present in the modern version, though there are exceptions such as the alleged ownership of the barn. Thus, Hanby's *Arminian Magazine* homily continues to provide the basic framework for the story as it is told today. However, the modern variant contains many details that are absent from Hanby (1785), mostly concerning the couple's identities, backgrounds and journey to the Winnats, and those elements alter the focus of the story. Also, the Divine justice theme that is central to Hanby's account is replaced in the online version by 'poetic' or 'natural' justice, and has become almost incidental to the plot. Finally, while that justice theme is the only 'supernatural' element in Hanby (1785), the other two elements – the precognitive dream and the ghosts of the murdered couple – are evident in the more recent telling.

Elements that are identical in the two accounts
1. The couple came from Scotland.
2. The murderers dragged them from their horses.
3. They took them to a nearby barn.
4. James Ashton confessed the crime on his deathbed and named the other murderers.
5. He had bought horses with his share of the booty but they all died.
6. The murderer Thomas Hall hanged himself.
7. The murderer Francis Butler went mad.

Elements in partial or close agreement between the two versions

Element	Hanby (1785)	Online version
1.	Date of incident *circa* 1758?	Date explicitly 1758
2.	Couple assumed to be on 'matrimonial expedition'	Couple going to Peak Forest to be married
3.	The murderers ambushed the couple 'at the Pass'.	The miners ambushed the couple half way through the Pass.
4.	The gentleman's throat was cut from ear to ear.	'Allan' was beaten to death.
5.	The lady was killed with a pick.	'Clara' was killed with pickaxes.
6.	The murderers returned after dark to bury the victims but were too afraid, and this was repeated on a second night.	The murderers returned after dark and buried of the bodies.
7.	The murderers shared out the money (£200) *after* they had buried the bodies.	The murderers shared out the money (£200) *before* they disposed of the bodies.
8.	The murderer Nicholas Cock fell from a precipice near the scene of the crime.	The murderer Nicholas Cook fell from a buttress.
9.	The murderer John Bradshaw was killed by a falling rock near the scene of the crime.	The murderer John Bradshaw was killed by a falling rock.
10.	The fates of the murderers showed the Hand of God.	The fates of the murderers were natural or poetic justice.

Elements that occur in Hanby (1785) but not the online version
1. The barn belonged to one of the murderers.
2. The lady pleaded for her companion's life.
3. She said she was the cause of his coming into that country.
4. On the third night after the murders, Ashton said that the frightening noises were 'only the Devil' and the bodies were then buried.
5. He said that the lady they had killed was the fairest he ever saw.

Elements that occur in the online version but not in Hanby (1785)
1. The couple were named Allan and Clara.
2. They had run away because of family opposition to their marriage (owing to disparity of wealth).
3. They stayed overnight at an inn in Stoney Middleton.
4. 'Clara' had a precognitive dream of the tragedy.
5. The dream was attributed to the weariness of the journey.
6. The couple travelled to Castleton and stopped at another inn.
7. A group of miners at the inn saw them and inferred that they were wealthy.
8. The miners heard the landlord direct the couple to Peak Forest via the Winnats Pass.
9. They decided to ambush and rob the couple at the Winnats.
10. On the way there they were joined by another friend.
11. 'Allan' pleaded for his own and his companion's lives.
12. The couple's horses were found on the fourth day after the murder.
13. The saddle belonging to 'Clara' is now in the Speedwell Cavern shop.
14. The ghosts of the murdered couple now haunt the Winnats Pass.

When and from what sources did these additional elements originate? We shall find some answers in five further variants of the tale that were recorded during the first half of the nineteenth century.

3

Other Early Variants

Hutchinson (1809)

Early in the nineteenth century, John Hutchinson of Chapel-en-le-Frith wrote a version of WPM that closely followed Hanby (1785). Hutchinson does not seem to have been associated with Methodism, so Hanby's rendering had presumably spread outside the new denomination by the early nineteenth century. *Hutchinson's Tour through the High Peak of Derbyshire* is a delightful book, evoking the scenery, the inhabitants and the difficulties of travelling around the Peak District during the early years of the nineteenth century in a clear, straightforward and often amusing way; though the author occasionally launches into rather inept poetry. The following excerpt is taken from an early part of the book, where the Castleton area is described.

At this place the most dreadful murder was perpetrated that has ever been recorded. About fifty years ago, a young lady and gentleman, returning from Gretna Green upon a matrimonial expedition, were attacked here by five ruffians, called Nicholas Cock, Thomas Hall, Francis Butler, John Bradshaw, and James Ashton, who seizing their horses, caused them to dismount, and dragging them into a barn, robbed them of two hundred pounds. Not satisfied with this booty, they then declared to the young lady their intention of murdering her lover. The lady was described by Ashton to be extremely handsome. But beauty in vain solicited their adamantine hearts; the supplications of the unhappy sufferers might as well have been addressed to the rocks which surrounded them. Without hesitation they immediately cut the throat of the gentleman, from ear to ear! And one of the monsters, if possible, more inhuman than the rest, being anxious to stop the piercing cries of the lady, took up a miner's pick, and in one moment, terminated her misery, by striking it into her head, and leaving her a lifeless corpse by the side of her lover.

The bodies of the sufferers were yet to be disposed of, and at the still and solemn hour of midnight, the villains met at the place of murder, for the purpose of burying them; but the never failing sting of conscience began to operate:– the most frightful noises were heard on every side, and they retired alarmed, and without accomplishing their object. They met at the same place on the second night, and returned equally dismayed, without fulfilling their intentions. But on the third night, Ashton, summing up his courage, declared to his companions in iniquity, that he believed what they heard was only the devil, who he was sure would do him no harm. They then removed and buried the bodies, which were found about ten years afterwards by some miners, who were sinking a shaft.

It is remarkably singular that all the above murderers came to an untimely or miserable end. Nicholas Cock fell down a precipice near the place of murder. Thomas Hall became a suicide. Francis Butler often attempted to commit the same crime; but being prevented, he at last died in a state of raging madness. And, wonderful to relate, as John Bradshaw was passing near the place where the bodies were buried, a great stone fell down, and killed him instantaneously on the spot. – James Ashton survived; but at length he was struck with remorse on his bed of sickness:– he seemed to be in the agonies of death for ten weeks; nor could he quit his miserable existence on earth, until he had made full confession of the whole of this barbarous deed. – Death then gave him the fatal blow.

Thus the untimely end of innocence was avenged by the never-failing hand of retributive justice; and the punishment of human laws, though seldom ever evaded, was supplied by that watchful eye which never can be deceived.

Hutchinson's writing is not overly flowery, but there are occasional instances of Gothic phrasing and hyperbole (beauty in vain solicited their adamantine hearts ... being anxious to stop the piercing cries of the lady ... leaving her a lifeless corpse by the side of her lover ... at the still and solemn hour of midnight ... death then gave him the fatal blow ... the untimely end of innocence ... a state of raging madness ... a great stone fell down). The contrast in style shows how spare and direct was Hanby's version, consistent with the Puritan roots of Methodism. The substantive differences between Hutchinson's and Hanby's variants are as follows:

1. The couple were 'returning from Gretna Green' and therefore presumably already married[1]. By 1809, runaway marriages were no longer possible at Peak Forest, but Gretna Green had achieved

national notoriety. Why they were 'returning' via the Winnats is not explained, since they were strangers to the area, but Hutchinson's claim has an interesting implication: they must have been travelling down the pass, i.e. towards Castleton. In that case, it is not clear how and when the murderers (mostly Castleton lead miners) had seen them and decided to ambush them. Most variants of the story presume that the couple were travelling in the opposite direction, i.e. westwards from Castleton.

2. The barn is not mentioned.
3. The couple were 'caused to dismount' rather than dragged from their horses.
4. The murderers told the lady that they intended to kill her lover; a particularly cruel twist in the tale.
5. The bodies were discovered about ten years *after the murders*, not ten years *before Ashton's confession*.[2]
6. The methods by which Hall committed suicide and Butler attempted suicide are not specified.
7. The 'frightful noises' are attributed to the murderers' pangs of conscience rather than to any supernatural agency, and Ashton's troubled conscience is made explicit in the closing sentences of the account.

Interestingly, although Hutchinson recounted the tale in his *Tour*, he did not mention it in his *Stranger at Castleton*, published a year later (Hutchinson, 1810). He may have been reluctant to offend local sensibilities further (cf. Flindall, 2005).

Jewitt (1815)

A different slant was taken by Arthur Jewitt of Rotherham, one of the many lesser poets who sought to emulate the narrative-verse achievements of Burns, Coleridge and Byron. Jewitt's *Henry and Clara, a Peak Ballad* formed part of his Romantic epic *The Wanderings of Memory* (Jewitt, 1815). No doubt he drew on local oral tradition – he knew the Peak District well – but most of *Henry and Clara* is surely his invention. In the poem itself, only the prefatory lines prove conclusively that it is a variant of the legend:

> Down tow'rds the WINNETS through whose darkling shade,
> The trav'ller hastes, admiring, though afraid,
> Around, the whirlwind sports in wild career,

High o'er his head impending cliffs appear,
So proudly frowning o'er the cumbent cloud,
Which wraps the valley in its misty shroud,
And hides each jutting crag's fantastic form,
The seeming work of some convulsive storm,
When a rude earth-quake cleav'd its wid'ning way,
And op'd her secret chambers to the day.
These rocks have been with human blood distain'd,
Here murder horrible, has silent reign'd,
Here plung'd her steel unseen by human eye,
And drown'd in death her haples victims cry. [sic]
Perchance some rustic will the tale relate,
Sacred to love and beauty's dismal fate,
And show the rock up which in wild despair,
Shrieking for succour ran the frantic fair,
Then bless his sinful soul, with rueful face,
And haste affrighted from the dismal pla*ce*.

He dates the murders at 1768, perhaps influenced by Davies's *New Historical and Descriptive View of Derbyshire*, published four years before *The Wanderings of Memory* (see chapter six).

> Henry and Clara
> A Peak Ballad
>
> Christians, to my tragic ditty,
> Deign to lend a patient ear;
> If your breasts e're heav'd with pity,
> Now prepare to shed a tear.
>
> Once there liv'd a tender virgin,
> Virtuous, fair, and young was she,
> Daughter to a wealthy lordling,
> But a haughty man was he.
>
> Many suitors rich and mighty
> For this beauteous damsel strove;
> But she all their offers slighted,
> None could wake her soul to love,
>
> One alone, of manners noble,
> Yet with slender fortune bless'd,

Caus'd this lady's bosom trouble,
Rais'd the flame within her breast,

Mutual was the blissful passion,
Strong and stronger still it grew,
Henry lived but for his Clara,
Clara but her Henry knew,

But alas! their bliss how transient,
Earthly joy but leads to care:
Henry sought her haughty parent
And implor'd his daughter fair.

Dar'd to ask the wealthy lordling
For the damsel's willing hand, –
Pleaded with respectful fervour,
Who could his request withstand?

Clara's father – he withstood it,
He the ardent suit denied, –
To a house so poor, though noble,
Never would he be allied.

Bade him seek a love more equal,
Banish Clara from his mind,
For he should no more behold her, –
She, – poor maid, he close confin'd,

Hapless Henry, thus rejected,
Lost, unfriended, and forlorn,
Wretched, sad, by all neglected,
His fond heart with anguish torn.

Then, to crown his bossom's sorrow, [sic]
News was whisper'd in his ear,
Clara on the coming morrow,
Would a lordling's bride appear.

Wild, distracted, mad with phrenzy,
To the father's house he flew,
There determined to behold her,
And to breathe his last adieu.

Joyous on the nuptial even,
Round the sparkling festal board,
With a crowd of guests carousing,
Sat this rich and haughty lord.

Left a moment unattended,
Clara soon that moment seiz'd,
First to heav'n her sire commended,
Then fled from home, tho' weeping, pleas'd.

Henry gained the castle portal,
A footstep Clara's fears alarm'd;
She stops, – she lists, – they came, – fast panting
Henry caught her in his arms.

Now no time for fond endearments,
Swift on wings of love they fled;
Till from father's house far distant,
Father's frowns no more they dread.

Then before the sacred altar,
They in wedlock join'd their hands:
Long their souls had been united
In indissoluble bands.

Now with virtuous rapture burning,
Whilst fond hope encreas'd the flame;
Tow'rds their home again returning,
To this lonesome place they came.

Christians, shall I close my story?
Words can never tell the tale; –
To relate a scene so bloody,
All the pow'rs of language fail.

In that glen so dark and dismal,
Five ruffians met this youthful pair;
Long the lover bravely struggled,
Fought to save his bride so fair.

But at last, o'erpowr'd and breathless,
Faint he sinks beneath their pow'r;

Joyful shouts the demon Murder,
In this gloomy midnight hour,

Bids them not to rest with plunder,
But their souls with rage inspires,
All their dark and flinty bosoms,
With infernal malice fires.

High they lift the murd'rous weapon,
Wretches hear ye not her cries?
High they lift the murd'rous weapon?
Lo! her love, her husband dies!

Rocks, why stood ye so unmoved?
Earth, why op'dst thou not thy womb?
Lightnings, tempests, did ye slumber?
Scap'd these hell-hounds instant doom?

High they lift the murd'rous weapon,
Who can 'bide her piercing shriek?
'Tis done – the dale is wrapt in silence,
On their hands, her life-blood reeks.

Dark and darker grows the welkin,
Through the dale the whirlwind howls;
On its head the black cloud low'ring,
Threat'ning now, the grey rock scowls.

Conscience, where are now thine arrows?
Does the murd'rer feel the smart?
Death and Grave, where are your terrors?
Written in the murd'rer's heart.

Yes, he sees their ghastly spectres
Ever rising on his view;
Eyes wide glaring, – face distorted,
Quiv'ring lips of livid hue,

Ever sees the life-blood flowing,
Ever feels the reeking stream,
Ever hears his last weak groaning,
Mingled with her dying scream.

Christians, I have told my ditty,
If you shudder not with fear,
If your breast can glow with pity,
Can you now withhold a tear?

There is no apparent commonality with Hanby (1785), though Jewitt probably knew Hanby's work since his native Rotherham was a hotbed of Methodism. A narrative poem suited to early nineteenth century taste could hardly resemble a stark Methodist sermon on the theme of Divine judgement. Apart from the obvious difference between flowery Romantic verse and spare, direct prose:

1.   Jewitt names the couple, not their murderers: his focus is on 'Henry' and 'Clara' and their tragic fate, not on their assailants – though the troubled consciences of the latter are evoked in the closing stanzas. The names 'Henry' and 'Clara' might have arisen in local tradition but could equally well have been Jewitt's inventions.

2.   Like Hutchinson, Jewitt presumes the couple were already married when they were robbed and murdered, though Gretna Green is not mentioned. They are travelling east (down the Winnats Pass), not west.

3.   The reason assumed for the couple's supposed elopement is a familiar Romantic cliché, which Hanby and Tregortha would have repudiated. Whether Jewitt created that background out of whole cloth, or gleaned it from the more sentimental purveyors of a local oral tradition, is uncertain.

4.   'Henry' fights the assailants while 'Clara' is passive – a conventional arrangement, but diametrically opposed to Hanby (1785).

5.   In accordance with Romantic principles, the local weather responds appropriately to the murders. The poet upbraids the surrounding landscape for failing to do likewise.

6.   The Divine Retribution theme is absent from *Henry and Clara*.

7.   However, we see a hint of the third 'supernatural' element of modern variants: the murderer sees 'ghastly spectres ever rising to his view'. No doubt Jewitt was emphasising the killers' pangs of conscience, but those lines seem to contain the germ of what would subsequently become, in part, a ghost story.

Nevertheless, Jewitt provided an explanatory note in *Wanderings of Memory* that largely reflected Hanby's account, though it added new details, particularly the discovery of the couple's horses. This explanatory note, together with *Henry and Clara*, was later reproduced by the poet's brother, Llewellyn Jewitt, in his *Ballads and Songs of Derbyshire* (Jewitt, 1867):–

In the year 1768, a young lady and gentleman, each mounted on a fine horse, had been up to the chapel of Peak Forest to be married, (as being extra-parochial, the Vicar at that time enjoyed the same privileges as the parson of Gretna Green, and married any couple that came to him, without making any impertinent inquiries concerning them,) and on their return, wishing to take Castleton in their way home, and being strangers in the country, found themselves benighted at the Winnats ... Here they were seized by five miners, dragged into a barn, robbed of a great sum of money, and then murdered. In vain the lady sought them to spare her husband; vainly he strove to defend his wife. While one part of them were employed in cutting the gentleman's throat, another of the villains, stepping behind the lady, drove a pick-axe into her head, which instantly killed her. Their horses were found, some days after, with their saddles and bridles still on them, in that great waste called Peak Forest; and Eldon Hole was examined for their riders, but without effect. They were then taken to Chatsworth, (the Duke of Devonshire being Lord of the Manor,) and ran there as 'waifs,' but never were claimed, and it is said the saddles are yet preserved there. This murder, thus perpetrated in silence, though committed by so large a company, remained a secret till the death of the last of the murderers; but Heaven, ever watchful to punish such horrid wretches, rendered the fate of all the five singularly awful. One, named Nicholas Cock, fell down one of the Winnats, and was killed on the spot. John Bradshaw, another of the murderers, was crushed to death by a stone which fell upon him near the place where the poor victims were buried. A third, named Thomas Hall, became a suicide; a fourth, Francis Butler, after many attempts to destroy himself, died raging mad; and the fifth, after suffering all the torments of remorse and despair which an ill-spent life can inflict on a sinner's death-bed, could not expire till he had disclosed the particulars of the horrid deed.

Rhodes (1824)

Ebenezer Rhodes probably wrote his short account of the murders around 1820, though it was not published until a few years afterwards (see chapter one). On page 194 of his *Peak Scenery*, having rhapsodised about the magnificence of the Winnats Pass, he dismisses the tale:

The Winnats is not without a tale of horror. About sixty years ago, a gentleman and lady, mounted on single horses and unattended with servants, are said to have been murdered in this dreary pass. They were strangers in the country, and some circumstances induced the supposition that they were on a matrimonial excursion to the north. They were both young, and one of the men concerned in the murder stated the lady to be extremely handsome. The morning after this atrocious act, the horses belonging to these unfortunate persons were found in the neighbourhood of Castleton, without riders, but properly caparisoned for travel. Suspicion pointed to the crime that had been committed, and an enquiry took place, when, after a few days' search, the dead bodies were found in one of the holes in the sides of the Winnats. All attempts to trace out the perpetrators of this horrid deed were for a long time fruitless: they escaped the punishment of an earthly tribunal, but a singularly-calamitous fate attended them. They were five in number: only one died in his bed, who confessed to have participated in the crime, and as he was the last survivor, he told who were the companions of his guilt; two of them, working near where the murder was committed, were killed by the sudden falling of a part of the rock above them; the other two were the victims of different accidents, and the inhabitants of this district regard their premature deaths as awful instances of divine vengeance. Such is the tale of blood connected with the local history of the Winnats, and it is so circumstantially related, that the names of the men who were concerned in the commission of the crime are mentioned, and the manner of their death particularly detailed. This story I have told as it exists in the vicinity of the place, but the enquiries I have made into the accuracy of the narrative induce me to suppose it fabulous.

Rhodes (1824) was either unaware of Jewitt (1815) or chose to ignore the ballad. His version broadly follows Hanby (1785), though there are substantial differences: for instance in the ways in which the murderers died and in the location – and timing – of the discovery of the bodies, and in the assertion that the couple were heading 'to the north'. However, Hanby's 'Divine vengeance' theme is still clear: 'they escaped the punishment of an earthly tribunal, but a singularly-calamitous fate attended them'. The claim that 'the inhabitants of this district regard their premature deaths as awful instances of divine vengeance' indicates that the Hanby version had been assimilated into the local oral tradition, as suggested in chapter two. Like Jewitt (1815, 1867), Rhodes (1824) mentioned the discovery of the murdered couple's horses, apparently on the day after the murders rather than 'some days later'. In this account, the bodies of the victims were found 'after a few days' search, in one of the holes in the sides of the Winnats', not in an engine pit after an interval of several years. If an 'enquiry took place' it would seem to have been unproductive, and Rhodes does not tell us who is supposed to have conducted it, or where. No record of any such inquiry can be found.

The Suicide Cave, so called because a young couple ended their lives there around 100 years ago. It is a 'hole in side of Winnats', on the northern face of the pass near its foot.

The two most interesting features of the Rhodes version are first, the statement that 'this story ... exists in the vicinity of the place', and second, the conclusion that 'the enquiries I have made into the accuracy of the narrative induce me to suppose it fabulous'. The first feature confirms that the story was in oral circulation in the Castleton area by the second decade of the nineteenth century. The second deserves further comment.

Rhodes's scepticism might be justified, but he could have had ulterior motives for 'supposing the narrative to be fabulous'. His intention in writing *Peak Scenery* was to promote the Peak District as a beautiful place to visit, so he would not have wished to cultivate the belief that Castleton was a hotbed of robbers and murderers. Also, a tale of horror and bloodshed might not have appealed to many readers at that time. Gothic fiction had passed its early peak of popularity, though as the Romantic Movement advanced it would see a revival, giving rise to the Victorian 'penny dreadful' and to horror stories such as those of Edgar Allan Poe (Stephens, 2000; Gamer, 2006). Flindall (2005) suggests that Rhodes denied the truth of the story because he had been intimidated, presumably by descendants of the murderers (who by virtue of local inbreeding may have constituted much of the population of Castleton). That would seem consistent with Hutchinson's silence on the matter in his 1810 publication (see above). Nevertheless, Rhodes was not the only sceptic – see, for instance, Shawcross (1903).

Wright (1831)[3]

A substantially different account was written, about ten years after Rhodes', by Hannah Wright of Hathersage. She was a wealthy lady, a niece of the great artist Joseph Wright of Derby, and the 60-70 completed pages of her notebook show a deep interest in local history, particularly in events in the Peak District during the preceding century. Almost half of her book concerns the Jacobite rebellion. Her account of the Winnats Pass murders is an attempt to reconstruct historical fact, not to tell a romantic or 'fabulous' story or to convey a moral or religious message. It begins with a more or less verbatim copy of the 1829 *Derby Mercury* article[4] given in Appendix I. Wright introduces three footnotes into this copy:

- On p. 2, to 'one of the wretches struck ...' she writes: 'John Bradley struck the lady with a miner's pick, miners don't use a pike ... Mr Eyre.'
- On p.3, to 'a cupola upon the Sheffield Road ...', she writes: 'By Mitchelfields'. Mitchelfields lay below Mitchelbank on the south-eastern outskirts of Castleton, where the Siggate and Pindale Road climb the hill from the market square.
- On p. 3, to 'where the bodies were buried ...,' she writes: 'On the opposite side of the road'. In other words, she and her informants had identified the Speedwell Mine as the place of burial.

However, she obtained a different version of the story from William Eyre of North Lees Hall, who acted as a guide to visitors who were interested in local history and legends (Flindall, 2005), and from a friend called Miss Bradshaw:

A young gentleman and lady, supposed to be foreigners, stopped & dined at Castleton as it was getting dusk, they were advised to stay there all night, but they were determined to proceed; in going up the Winnats they were met by the five men above named, who dragged them off their horses into a barn on the right hand side going up about twenty yards from the road, & there murdered them; the Lady piteously implored them to spare the Gentleman's life, but they were inexorable. The next morning their horses were found grazing by the road side in Peak Forest

Above and below: All that survives of the barn in which the murders are said to have been committed are these very large cornerstones, now serving as gate-posts. The white building in the background is the Speedwell Cavern shop, a little over 100 yards away from the barn site.

about three or four miles off, which led to the discovery of the murders. The Lady was richly dressed, her habit being laced with silver; fifteen years afterwards the blacksmith's daughter wore the habit. The horses became the property of the Lord of the Manor[5]; John Eyre, Mr Eyre's brother in law, remembered seeing them grazing in the Park when he went to work at Chatsworth, at the time he was an apprentice at Bubnell; one of them was a pie bald horse. John was 12 years older than Mr Eyre, who was born 9 May 1752, & says the murder was committed before he was born, but he has heard it talked of ever since he can remember.

The men were all miners, except Francis Butler who was a blacksmith & lived at Hope; he was going to sharpen their tools when he met the men just as they were seizing their victims, & was with them when the murders were committed; they were making a lime kiln, and in removing some lime stones that were under an old wall, they discovered the bodies. Thomas Marshall & his wife lived at Edale, were respectable people and had good memories, but there seems to be a mistake as to the time the murders were perpetrated; our late lamented friend Miss Bradshaw, gave us a similar account, & said it was during the rebellion in 1745, which agrees with Mr Eyre's statement; had it taken place in 1758, he would have been six years old at the time; in other respects the account is correct, but from the Lady & Gentleman going up the Winnats after they left Castleton, it appears they were going towards Scotland; it was never known who they were or from whence they came.

The recovery of the horses echoes Rhodes (1824), though like Jewitt (1867), Wright says that the animals were found near Peak Forest, which would not have been described as 'in the neighbourhood of Castleton'; it was a different mining liberty. Wright's is the earliest written account to state that the couple had dined in Castleton before venturing towards the Winnats, the first to indicate more or less precisely where the barn was located, and the first to state that one of the murderers (Butler) was a blacksmith. The description of the lady's dress is also a new detail: the lady and her murdered companion seem to have interested Wright – not as they interested Jewitt, but they are no longer incidental to the 'evil deed and Divine vengeance' theme of Hanby (1785). As in Rhodes's version, there is no mention of ownership of the barn, and scant detail about the murder itself. The information that 'John Bradley' (the 1829 *Derby Mercury*'s version of 'John Bradshaw') was the individual who killed the lady, and that Francis Butler's daughter subsequently wore the dress, is new and must presumably be attributed to Mr Eyre and/or Miss Bradshaw.

Wright's informants had apparently known the murder story from their earliest years, but a century had passed since the alleged event; memories and reports cannot be relied upon over so long a period. Therefore, the date of 1745 must be doubted. If it is correct, the conjecture that the couple were 'going towards Scotland' is perhaps plausible; the gentleman may have been associated with the Jacobite army. But Wright's ready acceptance of the date may only reflect her particular interest in the Jacobite rebellion.

There is no reason to doubt Wright's honesty, but her version contains questionable elements. First, the 'lime kiln' mentioned as the burial site cannot be identified. (It can hardly be the one on the old Sheffield Road, which was about a mile from the murder barn.) Second, it seems strange that the couple stopped to dine in Castleton and then set off on an unfamiliar and dangerous road after dark, against advice. Third, it would seem unusual for a blacksmith from a neighbouring village to arrive after dark to sharpen miners' tools[6]. Flindall (2005) draws attention to these cavils. However, the 'eye-witness' status of Wright's informants lends credence to the murder story as a historical event.

Anonymous Account in the Bagshawe Collection (undated)

The Bagshawe Collection in the Sheffield City Archives contains an unlisted file of manuscripts (Bag C/3363/11), bearing neither name nor date, that addresses several aspects of the history of Castleton and the surrounding area. The author clearly had a deep interest in local history and in documents relating thereto. It includes a distinctive account of the Winnats Pass murders. This manuscript begins with an almost verbatim copy of the 1785 *Derby Mercury* report[7] and continues, with inconsistent punctuation:

There is I believe another account of this affair in a book called the "Invisible World" and I think, it is mentioned in one of Wesley's books (The "News from the Invisible World" is one of Wesleys)[8] (Hunters Derb. Coll) no 53). Murders are long remembered and talked of in these regions. In 1756 a man & woman who were travelling on horseback were murdered at the Winyards near Castleton – The horses were valuable taken to Chatsworth as Waifs – It was never known who they were; nor by whom the deed was perpetrated, till in 1778 ('This year' says Mr Wilson who gives the account) a miner of Castleton called James Salt being near to his end acknowledged that he was one of five by whom the murder was committed. The four were dead – all by violent deaths but one – the man murdered was buried under some stones in Winyards Barn – Salt took the woman in a Sack to his house and kept her in a chest till a suitable opportunity and then buried her at the same place. Their bones were found when the barn was pulled down – Salt died half an hour after his confession Dec 1778. The booty was about £20 a man – A more particular account in Add MS6668 p. 895 – see above[9].

This unpublished manuscript conflicts with Hanby's account as follows:

1. The murderer who confessed in December 1778 was James Salt, not James Ashton. Salt is not mentioned in any published variant of the tale. No 'James Salt' appears in the Castleton Liberty mine reckoning books between 1752 and 1778 (the nearest approximation to the name is 'Jonathan Slate'), or in the Castleton parish registers for any time during the eighteenth century (DRO D1432 A/PI/1/1-2). The name therefore appears to be misleading – as is the name of Derby's newspaper of the period.
2. The booty was about £20 per man, i.e. about £100 rather than £200 *in toto.*
3. The bodies were buried in the barn where the murder was committed; the man's immediately, the woman's after an undefined interval during which she lay in a chest in Salt's house.

View down the Winnats Pass from above its summit (the western end), looking towards the Hope Valley and Castleton.

4. The incident occurred in 1756.
5. The remains were discovered when the barn was demolished. In principle, that need not contradict the 'digging of the engine-pit' or mine-shaft; the shaft at Speedwell was apparently surrounded by a high drystone wall, and a disused barn nearby could have served as a convenient source of dressed stone for that construction. However, the barn is clearly indicated in a parish survey of 1819 (DRO D911Z/P1-2), so it was certainly not demolished before the bodies were allegedly unearthed.[10]

The 'Mr Wilson' to whom the account is attributed cannot be identified, but because Hanby and the present anonymous author had two different informants, we have further confirmation that the story was generally known in the area and was in oral circulation at the time – as indeed this version states.

Overview

Collectively, these five versions suggest that:

• WPM remained in oral circulation in the Castleton area until at least the 1830s;
• the local inhabitants were reluctant to allow outsiders to tell the tale;
• it nevertheless attracted the interest not only of Methodists but also of local historians, promoters of early tourism and would-be Romantic poets.

At this stage, it is worth summarising the elements of the story as they appear in these diverse accounts. As we shall see in the next chapter, the best-known and most influential variant (Wood, 1843, 1862) drew on several of the sources explored in chapters two and three, and also on the continuing oral tradition.

In the following list, elements found in Hanby (1785) are indicated in bold type. (We recall that Wright (1831) also copied the 1829 *Derby Mercury* account, which is very close to Hanby's original: see Appendix I). The abbreviations are: H = Hutchinson (1809), J = Jewitt poem (1815), R = Rhodes (1824), W = Wright (1831), B = Bagshawe manuscript.

Murders occurred:	about 1758	H
	in 1768	J
	about 1760	R

in 1745	W
in 1756	B
Couple were called Henry and Clara	J
They were young	H, J, R, W
They were strangers in the area	W
They had eloped because Clara's father opposed marriage	J
Couple were returning: from Gretna Green	H
already married	J
They stopped to dine in Castleton	W
They were ambushed by five men at the Winnats	H/J
Murderers named as in Hanby	H, W*
Butler met the other four just before the ambush	W
Butler was a blacksmith; others were miners	W
They: caused the couple to dismount	H
dragged them from their horses	W
They took them to a barn	H, W
They robbed them of money	H £200; B £100
They declared their intention to kill the gentleman	H
Lady was richly dressed	W
Lady begged for gentleman's life	W
Couple begged for mercy	H
Gentleman fought the assailants	J
Gentleman's throat cut	H
One assailant killed lady with miner's pick	H
Storm broke after the murders	J
Murderers unable to bury bodies 1st or 2nd night	H
3rd night, Ashton said 'only the Devil' and bodies were buried in an engine shaft	H
– buried in the barn, the lady's after a delay	B
Horses found: near Castleton morning after murder	R
at Peak Forest morning after murder	W
Horses: became Chatsworth property	W
taken to Chatsworth as waifs	B
Murderers haunted by visions of dead victims	J
Bodies found: ten years later by miners sinking a shaft	H
a few days later in a hole in Winnats	R
under stones on site of lime-kiln	W
under stones in the murder barn	B
Deaths of murderers: as per Hanby	H
two killed by rock-falls, two by other accidents	R
four by violent deaths	B

Fifth murderer confessed on deathbed: Ashton	H
Salt	B

Ashton said the lady was very handsome	H, R
Butler's daughter later wore the lady's dress	W
Fates of miners were Divine judgment	H, R

* Wright has 'Bradley' for 'Bradshaw', as in *Derby Mercury* (1829).

Note that three elements in Hanby (1785) are missing from all the variants surveyed in this chapter: (1) the couple had come from Scotland; (2) the barn belonged to one of the murderers; (3) the lady said she was the cause of the gentleman coming into that country.

4

The Wood Version

English scholars began to collect folktales considerably later than their German and Scandinavian counterparts (see chapter seven). One of the earliest collectors in the Peak District was a self-taught local historian, William Wood of Eyam (1804-1865), the son of a local lead miner[1]. Employed during his youth as a silk weaver, Wood became fascinated by local history and was an assiduous collector of traditions. His first book, *The History and Antiquities of Eyam* (McCann, 1999; first published 1842), was an immediate success. In the wake of this publication, in the summer of 1843, the editor of the newly-established[2] *Buxton Herald and Gazette of Fashion* invited him to contribute a series of 'descriptive and historical sketches' to the newspaper.

The editor of the *Herald* knew his business. During the 1840s, Buxton was becoming increasingly popular as a spa and would soon be second only to Bath (see chapter one). The newspaper was therefore read not only by literate residents of the area but also, importantly, by the numerous summer visitors to the town. Many of those visitors were wealthy, educated and well read, and they had time on their hands. Several were no doubt eager for local information and for Good Stories with a local flavour. Wood was an excellent choice of contributor for that purpose; he gave the readers what they wanted.

In particular, he devoted four successive *Buxton Herald* articles to a highly melodramatic account of the Winnats Pass murders. Founded on Hanby (1785), this serial exploited other earlier sources, including Jewitt (1815), as well as local informants. But it was much longer than other variants, padded with elaborate detail (much of it obviously the author's invention) and written in the Victorian 'penny dreadful' style, which suited contemporaneous taste: pantomime villains ('heartless murderers', 'savages', 'miserable wretches'), flawless hero and heroine, overblown

Chantrey engraving showing Eyam, the birthplace of William Wood, in the early nineteenth century.

language, and scenes that remind us, anachronistically, of black-and-white horror films (thunderstorm illuminating corpses, burial by the light of a single lantern). Wood's readers would have relished this manner of story-telling. Not surprisingly, his version of the tale became popular, and because some of Buxton's summer visitors took their copies of the *Herald* away with them, it became known not only throughout the Peak District but also in other parts of the country. Wood's entire account, with only minor changes from the *Buxton Herald* series, was subsequently published as a short book (anonymous and undated), and was then included as the second chapter of his *Tales and Traditions of the Peak* (Wood, 1862). It has influenced most subsequent variants of the folktale.

However, it was not appreciated in Castleton. Wood (1862) remarked:

> I was surprised that my good neighbours of Castleton should have been a little chagrined on the first appearance of this tale in print: I am certain it cannot affect their material interests.

Perhaps not; but by that time, the lead mining industry was dying and Castleton, already a poor community, had become seriously impoverished and remained so until the tourist trade attained real economic significance after the 1890s[3]. The 'material interests' of Wood's 'good neighbours of Castleton' were therefore in a parlous state. According to Shawcross (1903, p. 15), their 'chagrin' was expressed unequivocally:

> In 1863 [sic], William Wood barely escaped maltreatment at the Nag's Head in consequence of his dramatic treatment of the story, in his Tales and Traditions of the Peak, 1862; the landlord, Samuel Royse, took him into another room, through the window he made a speedy exit, and quitted Castleton in haste.

Perhaps the people were 'chagrined' because Wood had profited from a story about them while they remained in dire poverty, or because he had cast aspersions on their communal rectitude – or, conceivably, because he told enough of the truth to hurt them.

Although to the twenty-first century reader Wood's style seems overblown to the point of risibility, and although there are some careless errors in his writing, his *Buxton Herald* series is manifestly the work of an intelligent, well-informed and shrewd story-teller. The later (1862) version is well known, but the original series has apparently never been reproduced since it appeared in 1843. The present chapter copies this *Urtext* in full. Comments are made on each of the four parts of the serial.

Buxton Herald 20(2), July 13th 1843

HISTORICAL & DESCRIPTIVE SKETCHES
OF
BUXTON AND ITS VICINITY
BY WILLIAM WOOD
No. V[4]
[Written expressly for the Buxton Herald]

THE SCOTTISH VICTIMS: OR THE MURDER IN THE
WINNATS, NEAR CASTLETON
Alas! the hapless pair in life's sweet bloom
Untimely met their dread appalling doom;
None to their weeping friends could e're relate
Where they had sudden fled, and what their fate.

The Buxton visitor will not, I opine, omit during his recreative visit to Castleton, spending an hour in the very singular chasm or dell, happily designated the Winnats, more correctly Windgates – or more poetically rendered, "the portals of the wind". "Happy! Happy! indeed," says some poet[5], "was the imagination that first suggested the name – 'the gates or portals of the winds.' " This wild ravine is bounded on each side by perpendicular rocks of an amazing height; yet it is not wholly devoid of beauty: numbers of rare and elegant plants picturesquely adorn the of the abyss, in other respects, deep, lonely, and dreary.

It is not a description of this long, winding and deeply interesting defile which is here intended; no: it is to give a few hitherto unknown particulars concerning a tale of blood connected with the local history of this ghost-haunted pass – the Winnats. To detail the particulars of a brutal and horrible murder, is not the most fascinating subject even for a juvenile writer; and, perhaps, far from being at all interesting to the general reader. But the story of the Winnats murder is full of circumstances of an extraordinary character: love on the part of the victims; awful ferocity of the murderers; and the most striking instance on record of Divine judgment! These and other minor attendant circumstances must be my apology for giving notoriety to a deed which has no parallel (taking all the particulars into consideration) in the annals of crime. Let me, however, just observe, that it is with some diffidence that I am about to lift the veil which has to the present hid in partial obscurity the minute particulars of this fearful tragedy: the more so as the perpetrators of the black crime, may have descendents or other kindred, who must necessarily wish all accounts of the dreadful crime to be henceforth buried in obscurity. In consideration of this, I will, in the sequent details suppress the names of the unfortunate actors in this tale of guilt – notwithstanding their being so well known about the Peak – and will distinguish them as follows: A.; B.; B-r; C.; and H.: they being five in number; and before commencing the story, let me fervently express the sincere hope that they have found that mercy in heaven, which they so barbarously refused to their trembling victims, after the most earnest and pathetic supplication that it is possible to be expressed in pitiful gestures and impassioned language.

About the middle of April, A.D. 1758, the then isolated inhabitants of Stoney Middleton, a small village near Eyam, and about twelve miles from Buxton, were more surprised than could scarcely be imagined now, at the arrival in the village, very early in the morning, in apparent great speed, of two very richly caparisoned, beautiful steeds; mounted by a tall and sprightly-looking, young gentleman, and a somewhat younger (and as the rustic villagers expressed themselves) "angel-like" looking lady. Their astonishment was increased by the fair strangers galloping up to the Royal Oak – an inn, if so called, of the village third degree. Arrived at the door they were soon dismounted; but not before they were encircled by a conclave of the home-spun-cloth clad village yonkers. who gazed

on the rich attire of the strangers, until their eyes bid fair for a trip from
their sockets. The gentleman rapped first gently then louder at the half-
open inn door, asking frequently for the hostler; when, after the lapse
of six or eight minutes, a girl about thirteen appeared, bearing evident
marks on her frontlet that she had been recently engaged in adjusting
the pot-hooks in the chimney. "The hostler!" repeated the gentleman.
"Mastur hasna nau oster," replied the browny, after having first cleared
her nasal pipes by taking three or four snuffs; each accompanied by a
shrug of the shoulders that that proved most satisfactorily that the two
steeds which stood very near had a full portion of that superior sagacity
for which horses have ever been characterised. The gentleman handed
his fair companion into a room, and immediately proceeded to assume
the office of hostler himself. During his short absence how did the lady
gaze around the room: tables, chairs, fireirons, coal-scuttles, and broken
pots were promiscuously squandered on the floor: satisfactory evidence
of the quality of the preceding night's company. Here lay a broken chair;
there a legless table, and other numberless mutilated domestic articles,
which had been the weapons and shields of the "pot-valiants" in the late
Bachanalian [sic] orgies. The lady sat in mute astonishment, for never
before that fateful journey had she seen such evidence of the great disparity
in the manners and modes of life. By the time the host and hostess had
descended from the realms of Morpheus; they entered the lady's room,
but almost involuntarily started back on beholding the costly garb, and
the entrancing beauty of their unexpected female guest. The gentleman
now rejoined his fair one, and having interrogated the hostess respecting
her articles of provision in the house, he briefly and politely apologised by
observing that he and his female companion would content themselves,
as their stay was so very short, with the little provisional delicacies they
had brought along with them, and would pass on to the next place for
breakfast. The two strangers were now alone in a room apart. The host
was in the kitchen corner chair hemming and swelling with pride at the
quality of his guests, fully persuaded that they had been recommended to
his house for its reputed respectability and accommodation. The servant
before alluded to, was busy among the dishes, and frequently one cried
smash upon the floor, occasioned by her imagining that she could feel in
the palm of her hand the shilling she should receive from the illustrious
guests. The wiley [sic] hostess was listening to the conversation of the
strangers through a lattice, which adjoined the room where they were
partaking of their repast. The prying dame had pinned up her mob cap
from over one of her ears which she kept as firmly fixed, and equally as
steady to the lattice as was the head of Sisera to the ground when pierced
by the nail of the heroic Jael[6]. According to the hostess, the lady did not

partake of the repast; but, to the gentleman's supplications for her to take some little refreshment, she only answered by deep heart-bursting sighs. The hostess also ascertained the gentleman's adopted name to be Allan; and the lady's, Clara: furthermore, she heard the following dialogue (next number) which, she averred, fixed her to the lattice in breathless fear: adding, that she could not understand all they said, for "sha thute tha wur fariners, tha tak'd sa quarely."

(To be continued.)

Since Wood is writing 'historical and descriptive sketches of Buxton and its vicinity', he begins with a description of the Winnats Pass and makes references to Buxton as a geographical centre. He then tells his readers that the story he is about to recount is the result of his own historical research, 'lifting the veil' on details of the murder story that have previously been suppressed. Thus he acknowledges his remit from the editor of the *Buxton Herald* and, at the same time, establishes his credentials as a local historian.

The Divine Vengeance theme of Hanby (1785) is explicit from the start, but the traditional names 'Allan' and 'Clara' for the murder victims appear for the first time in this account. Even if Wood is reporting what he had heard rather than inventing those names, we can see that the evidence for them is extremely tenuous. We have a 100-year-old report of what the eavesdropping landlady allegedly claimed to have heard through the lattice; and could she really have heard what she claimed? Although her ear was allegedly glued to the lattice, we must presume that the couple were speaking quietly, and since they were 'fariners', the listener is unlikely to have heard every word correctly. In any case, things heard and seen in the past are notoriously altered by memory and the passage of time, and Wood can only have heard the landlady's account at second or third hand. The dialogue supposedly gleaned from the same eavesdropping source (see below) is even more implausible – by a considerable margin. Wood may simply have adapted the names of the couple from Jewitt (1815), ostensibly 'correcting' the poet.

The couple's halt at Stoney Middleton is an entirely novel element in Wood's version. No earlier written account attests to it but Wood may have gleaned it from a continuing oral tradition. The Royal Oak was apparently a lawless place in the eighteenth century (Cowen, 1910), so the scene of devastation that greeted 'Clara' is credible. Therefore, even if Wood is being creative, he seems to circumscribe his inventiveness by acknowledging tradition and perhaps even fact.

Overblown though the writing style may seem to us, it is careless in places. The closely-linked statements '... where they were partaking of their repast ... the lady did not partake of the repast' are at once repetitive and contradictory; the spellings 'wiley' and 'Bachanalian' are idiosyncratic; Jael did not apparently nail Sisera's head to the tent floor; and the attempt to disguise the murderers' names is otiose, clumsy and probably disingenuous. Nevertheless, Wood writes cleverly and deploys the 'cliff-hanger' principle effectively: his readers must wait a week before they can read the dialogue that supposedly frightened the eavesdropping hostess of the Royal Oak.

Buxton Herald 21(2), July 20th 1843

HISTORICAL & DESCRIPTIVE SKETCHES
OF
BUXTON AND ITS VICINITY
BY WILLIAM WOOD
No. V. (CONTINUED)
[Written expressly for the Buxton Herald]

———

THE SCOTTISH VICTIMS: OR THE MURDER IN THE
WINNATS, NEAR CASTLETON
"O, I have pass'd a miserable night,
Sated of dreams – of ugly sights, –
* * * * *
I would not spend another such a night,
Though 'twere to buy a world of happier days:
So full of dismal terror was the tune." – *Shakespeare.*

In my last, I left the worthy hostess of the Royal Oak Inn, listening intensely to the conversation of her stranger guests, which – excepting the liberty I have taken of giving it unadorned by the High Derbyshire brogue of the hostess – was nearly as follows:-

ALLAN – "Clara, my dear, pardon me for saying that I imagine I have perceived, during this morning's ride, a shade of despondency upon your angel brow; pray, let me hear if aught, – ah! if even a thought – disturbs your mind, that I may willingly bear the suffering it occasions."

CLARA – "Ah! my Allan, your anxious gaze has long bespoken some interrogation; but, alas! what weighs so heavy at my heart, cannot! cannot be alleviated by human sympathy."

ALLAN – "Come, my adored, my ever dearest Clara, come tell me what it is that has produced this change in your till now soul-gladdening countenance? Surely your love has not, during our journey, suffered the least diminution?"

CLARA – "Allan, my faithful Allan, speak not of impossibilities. Do you forget the numberless expedients which have been used to estrange my affections from you; but in vain. Let me now tell you that, on the night I left my father's house to meet you to escape to England, I more than fully proved the intensity of my love! Ah! that evening! that evening! I sat beside my father, whose eye, methought, almost discovered our secret in my face. Jocund were my dear brothers and sisters, while I, feigning illness, early retired to bed; but not to sleep. When midnight came, the appointed hour, I arose; my sisters, sleeping, I kissed again and again, and left their cheeks suffused with tears. Softly I stole into my parent's [sic] room! I stood beside their bed, and sighed, farewell, farewell! O! never can I forget the conflicting emotions that, during those few moments, rent my soul. I saw, in imagination, my aged parents aroused from their slumber in the morning by the wailings of my sisters, 'O! father! O! mother! our Clara's gone! our Clara's fled!' The consequent distraction which I imagined had almost compelled me to retract from my vow, when I heard your signal, and in a moment I was in your arms. Allan! my Allan! why doubt the unchangeability of my love?"

ALLAN – "Then why this change which I have so painfully noticed this morning?"

CLARA – "Allan, I will tell you: 'tis a dream which I had last night: a dream so full of horror that the chilliness of death creeps through my soul at the thought of reciting it: yet I will essay. Methought that we alone were walking among some barren hills which I imagined, as we rode along this morning, much resembled those which we beheld in the distance. There was a stillness and strangeness in the scene which affected me most peculiarly as we walked along. After a while we descended a hill into a valley, the most romantic and picturesque that imagination can conceive. A rivulet was winding along the vale, singing a song of peace, most enchantingly delightful. In the centre of the valley we sat down on a daisy-decked knoll, reciprocally vowing the fervency of our affection and love. It was at this moment that I felt a consciousness of someone being near. I turned my head to the right, when lo! I saw a little brother of mine, who had been dead twelve years. I started with the most intense surprise: his countenance was pale and ghastly as when I saw him in his last moments; his eyes were fixed on me, with some kind of meaning in their expression, perfectly indescribable. A tremor agitated my frame as I attempted to call him by his name; however, I repeated his name twice, and the last time, he lifted up his ashey hand, pointed to the top of the opposite hill, shook his head and vanished. I then, absorbed in thought, looked for a while towards the little hill to which my brother had pointed; when I could perceive four or five distinct beings advancing towards us, yet I could scarce believe them to be human. Soon they reached us, and their terrific aspects made me tremble with horror; for although they were men, their garb, demeanour, and brutal countenances, induced me for awhile to think they were monsters unknown to mankind. Now, my dearest Allan, commenced the terrible scene which has left so deep and indelible an impression on my mind. Methought they seized us both, and hurried us away into a gloomy cavern, the interior of which filled me with the most painful horror imaginable. And what increased my agony to the uttermost was, I beheld them mangle your body in the most bloody and awful manner; then they did fix their deadly glance on me; and with a suffocating shriek I awoke, and for a while, with open eyes, I struggled hard with the dread phantoms of my dream."

ALLAN – " 'Twas horrid surely; but calm your mind, my love; dreams are only the freaks of fancy; which take their hue and character from circumstances, often, if not always, ideal and insubstantial."

CLARA – "Ah! my Allan, I fear! I fear not! that which has received the concurrent and universal testimony of mankind in all ages of the world, is entitled to some respect and credence. That some calamity awaits us, I have a most agonizing dread."

ALLAN – "Be comforted, my fond Clara – banish from your bosom such doleful thoughts. I have a thousand times over dreamed of our happy union in the bonds of matrimony; dreamed of leading you to the altar, and felt, during those blissful moments, an happiness that I should in vain attempt to describe: but which, I now hope, ere the sun sets behind the western hills, to enjoy in reality. Come, my Clara, take some little refreshment while I just speak to the host and see our horses in readiness."

The host and Allan were now in the stable, and Allan took the opportunity of asking the host a few questions – "How far is it to a place named the Forest of the Peak," said Allan; "why, about eight miles," replied the host. "What is the distance from there to Buxton," asked Allan; "not a many miles," said the host. "We shall go through Castleton to the Peak Forest, I suppose," said Allan. "Ah, belike, and then through the Winnats," replied Boniface. "Well, good host, you will bring the horses to the door, in a few minutes, will you?" "Ah, Sur! ah, Sur! I will," replied the polite and gentlemanly host. Allan again joined his fair one, who sat absorbed in thought; "come, my dear," said he, "we must away, the horses are ready – they will now mount the hills like Apollo's steeds, up heaven's steep." Clara rose from her seat and deeply sighed: a dark presentiment of evil was entwined round her heart; and her agitation greatly affected Allan, although he endeavoured to conceal it from her notice. Soon they were mounted on their fleet-footed coursers;

and very quickly were out of sight. A few villagers had been conning the strangers anent the Inn, to whom, when the strangers were gone, the host approached, and thus immediately vociferated, "Na, I'st bet ony one on ya my new drab-coat-cloth that yon two are for a Gretna Green job, thu are for th' Peak Forest, and yo known jobs a that sort is done thare welly same as Gretna-Green"

   The hapless pair are now wending their way to Castleton, where they intend stopping a short time. Allan looks with wonder at the lanigerous vales and the manifold mist-capt hills which bound their view on every side; Clara rides by his side, silent and thoughtful; her bosom heaves at intervals with bursting dispair [sic]; unconsciously, with trembling hands, she guides the rein; for, ah! her thoughts are full of that fell dream,
"And through her veins a chilling terror glides." – Tasso.
(To be continued.)

In complete contrast to Hanby (1785), but in the spirit of Jewitt (1815), Wood is engaging the reader's sympathy with the doomed couple, particularly with 'Clara'. He has given them names, which is a *sine qua non* for such sympathy; he has emphasised their undying mutual love; and although their supposed dialogue is absurdly melodramatic, it contrives to portray 'Allan' as practical and energetic, and 'Clara' as sensitive, reflective and in need of protection, as a Victorian heroine should be. Like Jewitt (1815), he bestows an unsympathetic father on Clara, and he also provides her with mother, brothers and sisters.

   One important novelty in this episode is the second of our three 'supernatural' features: the precognitive dream. The details of this so closely match the events of the subsequent murder as to render it transparently spurious; but given the expectations of Wood's audience it was no doubt an effective device[7]. Also, as we have seen, it is compatible with the Methodist tradition of the story's origins (cf. Tregortha, 1806), of which Wood was clearly aware; a warning from a deceased relative is a common theme in early Methodist stories. The switch to the present tense in the final paragraph is another strong rhetorical device, driving the narrative forward towards its next exciting episode.

   However, there is something very odd about the directions to Peak Forest. The host tells 'Allan' that the distance is eight miles; and so it is if the route through Middleton Dale and past Tideswell is followed. But by going first to Castleton, then through the Winnats and back to Peak Forest, the couple were required to travel several miles further. Given the quality of the roads at the supposed time of the murder, that journey must have taken at least three hours and probably longer, particularly with the lady riding side-saddle[8]. Certainly the claim that the couple 'very

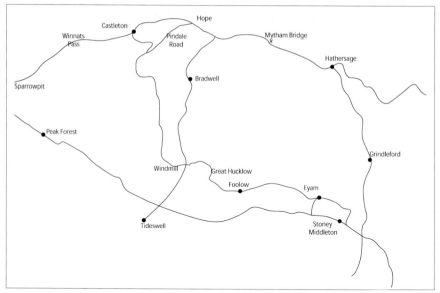

Sketch map showing the routes that the couple might have followed from Stoney Middleton to Castleton.

quickly were out of sight' is implausible. Wood – a native of Eyam, which is very close to Stoney Middleton – knew the routes thoroughly, but he neither tells us which way the couple travelled from Stoney Middleton to Castleton nor explains why they were sent on such a roundabout route to Peak Forest. Are we to suppose that the landlord misdirected his guests on purpose?

Wood finds it necessary to explain, using the landlord's voice, that Peak Forest could perform the same service as Gretna Green. The 'foreign marriage' arrangement had ceased altogether in Peak Forest at the beginning of the nineteenth century (Rogerson, 1901), so when Wood wrote his *Buxton Herald* series, few of his readers would have known about it; but they would all have heard of Gretna Green. At the supposed time of the murders, however, Gretna Green was a new innovation while there was a long-established tradition of 'foreign marriages' in Peak Forest. Given Wood's audience and his intentions, this deliberate anachronism is understandable.

Buxton Herald 22(2), July 27th 1843

HISTORICAL & DESCRIPTIVE SKETCHES
OF
BUXTON AND ITS VICINITY
BY WILLIAM WOOD
No. VI. (CONTINUED)
[Written expressly for the Buxton Herald]

———————

THE SCOTTISH VICTIMS: OR THE MURDER IN THE
WINNATS, NEAR CASTLETON
"All unavoidable is the doom of destiny." – SHAKESEPEARE.

It is a merciful dispensation of providence that, a foresight or knowledge of the tragical ends or termination of life, to which numbers are doomed in all countries, is impenetrably veiled from their mental vision until the almost actual transpiration. Indeed, were it otherwise, human existence would be insupportable; a torrent of dispair would overwhelm and utterly destroy those mental emenations [sic] which so unequivocally evince the glory and wisdom of the great author of our being. It is, however, difficult to account for the opinion which has been held with tenacity by such great numbers, that they have had prognostications of their fates; presages of their and others' tragical destinies; and in a manner convincingly impressive. By the especial interposition of providence alone, can this opinion be accounted tenable; and when providence does interpose cannot be determined infallibly by the evidence of human testimony.

There was, however, something in the dream of Clara, as we shall see hereafter, strikingly coincident with the fate of herself and her unfortunate lover. Her despondency increased during their journey from Stoney Middleton to Castleton, which was about nine miles[9]; a journey amid mountains which wore their unchanging garb of thousands of years; mountains mist-capt, whence men may,

"Look down
On towns that smoke below, and homes that creep
Into the silvery clouds, which, far off keep
Their sultry state! and many a mountain stream,
And many a mountain vale, and ridgy steep;
The Peak, and all his mountains, where they gleam
Or frown, remote or near, more distant than they seem."
ELLIOTT.

It was near ten o'clock of the fateful day when the unfortunate pair reached the village of wonders – Castleton; they rode up at a brisk pace to one of the Inns, but not the principal; this plan they had, besides taking a circuitous rout [sic], invariably adopted during their journey: a necessary expedient to avoid being traced and overtaken by Clara's father and brothers, who had the most inveterate antipathy to Allan. They alighted from their smoking steeds at the Inn-door, and were shown into a room somewhat more respectable and comfortable than that at the Royal Oak, Stoney Middleton. Allan, after having ordered the horses to be stabled and fed, called for breakfast to be served with the greatest dispatch. Clara took her seat in a corner of the room, leaned her head against the wall, and deeply sighed; Allan placed himself by her side, and in the most endearing, loving, and pathetic language he could command, conjured her to raise her drooping spirits; and then, in the glowing colours of heartfelt affection, portrayed the years of unalloyed happiness with which they should be henceforth blessed. The earnest exhortations of Allan aroused Clara to some degree from her death-like stupor; she turned her head, gazed him steadfastly in the face, until the burning tears

"Rushed from her clouded brain,
Like mountain mists, at length dissolved to rain." – BYRON.

Breakfast was served, and Allan was in the act of endeavouring, in the most kind and persuasive language he could summon to his aid, to induce his Clara to partake, when an opposite room-door was thrown open, and he beheld, with some emotion, five uncouth, savage-looking men seated round a table, evidently in a state bordering on inebriation. While he looked on them with some surprise, one, seemingly by his glaring eyes the most intoxicated, broke out, in a voice rough as his garb and nature, with an attempt to mouth or sing the following doggrel [sic] lines:-

"Come fellows drink – drink, drink your fill,
Full soon we mu-t [sic] gang up the hill,
Where Odin rich in shining ore
Shall give us glasses – hundreds more:
The luck to Odin, – golden mine,
With metal bright, like th'sun doth shine."

The last couplet was a sort of chorus, in which they all joined with a bawl so loud, that "roof an' rafters a' did dirl." The worthy host now appeared among them, and thus politely vociferated: "As you've been these five days and netes, fellows, and as youy [sic] now begun a wanting to chalk, I'd rather you'd mizzle – I've a lady and gentleman ith' parlour, so bounce!" On this they all arose; swung their groove-clothes on their backs – gave the landlord a hearty curse, and reeled out of the house. Staggering down the village they went; calling, however, at all the other Inns; but at every one of which they met the door "slap bang" in their faces, accompanied by the significant exclamation, "go where you've been, sots!"

These drunken Bacchanalians (the initials of whose names as mentioned in the commencement of this narrative, were A-; B-; B-r; C-; H-, now repaired towards Odin, where they were employed – a mine that was worked, as its name imports, in the time of the Danes: a thousand years ago. It is about a mile north-west of Castleton: and it was on the way thither that the following criminous conversation transpired among the five miners alluded to – conversation darkly ominous: – "I sey, chaps," said A –, "what did ye think about th' old d-l of a landlord, t'order us awey becase [sic] we'd no money, and he'd better company ith' parler?" "Why," replied B-r, "I didna think sa mich about that as about summut else as crost my ene." "What's that, old buck?" asked C–; "Nay, nout very mich," replied B-r. "Na, I know, as sure as Mam Tor and that old Castle, what B-r means." H– immediately exclaimed. "Wa, what is it? what the d-l is it?" said B–. "Ah! out weet! out weet," said A–, "wear aw one, aint us?" "Belike, belike," rejoined B–; "well na, if B-r al not deny it, I'll guess, and guess reet," H– said immediately. "Come, then, at it," the other four replied. H– then commenced, and said, "na, B-r, didst than a see the gentleman with the lady, tak saddle bags off his horse at th' inn door, an didst na think they were full a money, they seemed sa heavy; an didst na think tha shud like sum of it?" "Well, I did, lad," replied B-r; "an if yoan amind, we'll go o'er th' hill here, an meet em ith' Winnats, an tak it on um – they'll go up there, I'm sure." After a little more altercation, they agreed to B-r's proposal, and they wended away swiftly towards the Winnats.

The sun was near its meridian height, when Allan and Clara left Castleton. Rapidly they rode along into the Winnats; but what pen can describe the agonising fear of Clara, when on entering the most secluded part of the defile, up sprang the five human savages, and seized the bridles of their horses, and with horrid imprecations bade the riders to dismount. Allan, with a countenance pale as death, looked towards Clara, who with quivering lips faintly ejaculated, "Allan, my dream! my dream!" H– and B– had hold of the bridles, while the other three paced round the horses and, with their pickaxes uplifted, swore that if they did not immediately dismount, they would bury the steel in the horses' heads, and after that, in theirs. Allan, in the most beseeching manner, said, "I hope, my friends, you intend no injury to two strangers. See! see!

the lady is falling from her horse with fear! Pray have mercy on us! spare our lives, and you shall take everything we have; but in mercy injure us no further, for this dear lady's sake!" "No cavil," said H-. and springing up, he seized Allan's cloak, and brought him screaming to the ground. "Somebody'll be coming; let's haul em into the barn, there," said B-; and they immediately hurried Allan away, piteously supplicating for mercy!

This done, they returned for Clara, whom they
"Dragged from among the horses feet,"
and carried her away, in a state of insensibility, to the same fearful and fatal place.
(To be continued.)

Once again there are idiosyncrasies of spelling and of punctuation, but the narrative remains consistent in style and character. The ill-fated lovers are identified only by their supposed forenames, the villains only by their crudely disguised surnames, and the minor actors in the drama by no names at all. Our sympathies and antipathies are ensured – the description of the miners serves only to gild the lily. Wood inserts a few verifiable facts into his account: for example, the distances from Stoney Middleton to Castleton and from Castleton to the Odin Mine are more or less accurate, and it was widely believed in the nineteenth century that the Odin Mine had been worked during the time of the Danelaw (it might indeed be true). The simulation of Derbyshire speech is generally plausible, and terms such as 'groove-clothes' to denote mining attire would be familiar to the local residents among Wood's readers; we recall that his father was a lead miner. His judicious sprinkling of such details lent verisimilitude to the blatantly invented parts of his narrative, such as the fictitious conversation among the miners.

We are given a somewhat lame explanation for the choice of route: the couple were trying to shake off possible pursuers. But in the previous episode we were told that the host of the Royal Oak directed 'Allan' to Peak Forest via Castleton; it was therefore not a deliberate choice by 'Allan'. Despite their stay in Stoney Middleton earlier in the morning and their subsequent ride of perhaps three hours, the lovers still managed to reach Castleton in time for breakfast, so either breakfast was very late or they made far better time than the roads would have allowed. The Castleton inn where they stopped is not identified[10], but we are told that it was not the hotel now known as the *Castle* (in times past it was called the *George* – now, confusingly, the name of the hostelry that was previously called the *Castle*), which was surely the 'principal'.

In Wood's later (1862) rendering of the tale, and in many of its modern derivatives, the number of miners in the inn is reduced to four. The fifth,

John Bradshaw, described here as a blacksmith at the Odin Mine, met the other four murderers some distance from the village and was only persuaded to join the scheme because the quartet threatened him with violence if he refused. The conversation among the miners *en route* from the inn is edited accordingly in Wood (1862). As we have seen, Wright (1831) tells us that Francis Butler, not John Bradshaw, was the blacksmith; and that John Bradshaw (or 'Bradley') cold-bloodedly and single-handedly murdered the female victim – scarcely the action of a man who took part in the crime only under compulsion (see below).

The site of the barn is not in 'the most secluded part of the defile' but close to its eastern entrance; here, Wood opts for poetic licence rather than accuracy. The miners deviated from their path to the Odin Mine to go 'over the hill here' to the point of ambush; this location will be discussed in chapter six.

'Allan' is more proactive than the gentleman in Hanby (1785), but he makes very little show of defending himself or 'Clara' against their assailants. Gentleman travelling through strange country in the eighteenth century carried arms and knew how to use them. 'Allan' might have been surprised and badly outnumbered, but pickaxes are clumsy weapons even in experienced hands and would have conferred no defence against pistols, and little against a sword. Neither Wood nor any other teller of the tale addresses this difficulty.

Buxton Herald 23(2), August 3rd 1843

HISTORICAL & DESCRIPTIVE SKETCHES
OF
BUXTON AND ITS VICINITY
BY WILLIAM WOOD
No. VII. (CONTINUED)
[Written expressly for the Buxton Herald]

———

THE SCOTTISH VICTIMS: OR THE MURDER IN THE
WINNATS, NEAR CASTLETON

"Did not Heav'n turn pale,
And the earth shudder to behold the beasts –
The worse than wolves? – O Nature, were they men?"

The awful suspense – the indescribable agony experienced by Allan, while four of the brutal savages were gone for Clara, language cannot portray! H– had been left to prevent Allan from escaping, or giving any alarm during the others' absence; and Allan, in this bitter extremity, would fain have won H– over by promises and tender supplications; but, the callous-hearted villain, who stood in the doorway of the barn, swore vehemently that if Allan moved one limb or spake one word more, he would bury his uplifted pickaxe into his body; on which Allan shuddered and said no more.

As the heartless murderers entered the barn with Clara, Allan received them on his knees, and, with his purse in his hand, said, "for Heaven's sake take this! take this! take our all, but O! in mercy spare our lives! do not, my dear friends, for that dear lady's sake, injure us any further! B– snatched the purse from Allan, while the other rifled his pockets. This done, they retired outside the barn to consult on further proceedings.

"I wish", said A–, "we'd na com'n at'e a Castleton t'dey; we's be fun at'e shure enough, an be hanged." "Wa," replied B-r, "if we are fun at'e, we's know ar doom; but we mun stop that, if we can." "Stop it! stop it!" exclaimed B–: "there's nought but one chance a that, na." "What's that?" asked C–. "Why," said H–, "he means t'kill 'em; and I'm it same mind." "I dunna like that," A– emphatically rejoined. "Well," H– swore, "if tha's qualms of conscience, we's be obleeged to do it arsels; an if wer fun at'e after, tha mun swing wa us – not for murder – but for company. Come, B-r, let's all into um, or shure we's be catched with horses standing yonder."

During this awful consultation, Allan had crept to Clara, whom he had by the most tender caresses brought back to sensibility. He endeavoured to persuade her that the worst was past; but, her wild gaze around the barn, and her faint ejaculations, "my dream, Allan! my dream!" filled his despairing soul with bitter agony. Returning footsteps now fell on their ears with all the terrors of immediate death. H– entered first; and Allan fell on his knees again and said, "O my friends! if you will but spare this lady's life, I will! I will with my own hands take mine before your eyes? Do not, I implore you, injure her, do what you will with me!" This heartrending appeal had little effect. The heartless wretches were busy about the door, – making fast inside, when Clara suddenly sprang from the corner of the barn where she had been laid, and in an attitude of humble prostration thus exclaimed, "If ever woman's tongue did raise a thought of pity – if ever sighs and tears could move the heart of mortal man, let me now beseech you, in pity to spare the life of my companion, my love, my Allan! 'Tis me! 'tis me! ah! 'tis through me alone, that we are here. Come, in this my naked bosom plunge that fatal knife: but, O! in mercy spare my loved, my dearest Allan." Clara as she finished this pathetic exclamation, closed her eyes, hung back her head, and presented her snow-white naked bosom to the savage monsters. Meanwhile, Allan, aroused by the moving appeal of Clara, sprang upon his feet, and rushed between her and the heartless murderers; a moment elapsed, and he, in the agony of despair, rushed towards the savages, seized B-r by the throat and dashed him to the ground. Then, with the fury of a tiger he sprang upon the others, who instantly surrounded him, and a struggle ensued that only the pencil of a Salvator Rosa[11] could portray. In a few minutes Allan was overpowered and fell: yet, against their united strength he had almost gained his feet again, when H– plunged the knife with which had entered the barn, into Allan's throat, and he fell gasping and bleeding to the ground. During the latter part of this awful struggle, the screams of Clara were terrific, to silence which B– seized a pickaxe and smote it into her head, and the two unfortunate victims, almost in the same moment, breathed their last. A stream of blood issued from each of the fatal lovers, and commingled together on the floor of the fatal barn. Silent and horror-struck the murderers looked on their victims as they lay stiffening with death, wishing intensely, when alas too late, they had spared their lives. Then it was that the enormity of their crime overwhelmed them with life-lasting anguish; then it was that blood-bought guilt stamped their accusing minds with the deadly seal of horror implacable. They gazed on each other in speechless awe; the beautiful form and features of Clara aroused their attention, for oh!

> "A form of wax,
> Wrought to the very life was there;
> So still she was, so pale, so fair." – MARMION.

These miserable wretches, who had died [sic] their hands with innocent blood, remained in the barn until the shades of evening chased the weary day from every mountain side. During their stay in the fatal place a violent thunderstorm occurred, which added immeasurably to their perturbation of mind. The lightning flashed on the bloody faces of their fated victims; the thunder rebellowed in the horrible dell, and the guilty murderers trembled with excessive fear. Conscience-stricken, they heard in every crack the appalling voice of justice calling aloud for vengeance, and worlds would they have given to have undone their bloody deed.

Night had approached when they divided their booty, which was £200 in money and other valuables. They stripped Clara of her outer silken vestment, and placing her beside the blood-clotted Allan, covered them with some unclean straw and retired, having first agreed to return to the barn at midnight and inter the bodies. Midnight came and they repaired to the solitary place; but their "blood guiltiness" peopled the shades of night with horrid forms; they heard in imagination the shrieks of woe, and they retreated in precipitation from the dismal place. The following night they ventured again; but on their arrival at the scene of blood, two steeds, each mounted by a spectre, with hair dabbled with gore, rushed by them, and entered the barn; on which they retraced their steps more terrified than before. On the third night they again repaired to the barn, determined on accomplishing their purpose; at the barn they heard the same dismal wailings of distress, and were about to return, when A– exclaimed – "it's only the d-l, he'll not hurt us," on which they entered; put the bodies in two sacks, and by the dim light of a solitary lantern, buried them at a little distance from the scene of their horrible death. This done, they return, but not alone: visibly they behold,

> "Two ghastly spectres,
> Ever rising to their view
> Eyes wide glaring – face distorted,
> Quiv'ring lips of livid hue." – JEWITT

The day following the interment of these hapless lovers, there [sic] horses were found, saddled and bridled, on the forest adjoining the Winnats; and when brought into Castleton, great surprise was thereby excited. The probability of the riders having been murdered and thrown into Elden Hole, was generally entertained; but, a descent into that fearful chasm, and nothing found appertaining to them, proved the supposition erroneous. The horses were, in due time, removed from Castleton to Chatsworth as waifs; the Duke of Devonshire being tenant to the Duchy of Lancaster, for the manorial rights of Castleton. – About ten years after this circumstance, some miners in removing some earth to sink an engine shaft, discovered two skeletons, which were generally believed to be those of the gentleman and lady who belonged to the horses: this was further corroborated by one of the skulls having all its teeth perfect except one in the front, a deficiency which had been observed in Allan, both at Castleton and Stoney Middleton. The skeletons were buried in the church-yard at Castleton, but no clue of the murderers could then be discovered. After the discovery of these human remains, there were, now and then, a few dark hints dropped respecting the supposed guilty persons: originating, chiefly, in the sudden change in the circumstances of the suspected individuals, and in words spoken by them in unguarded moments. A– bought horses with his share of the booty, but they died in rapid succession; and, when on his journeys, he frequently said, "I have always a beautiful lady with me – she rides on my horse." C-'s daughter went to the Church often in a very rich silk dress, which excited the notice of the whole village. As no inquiry was ever made after the two unfortunate lovers, there was no possibility of ascertaining who the perpetrators of the murder were, except by the voluntary confession of one or all of the murderers; which, as the reader will see, was the case with A-.

Though the hand of human justice did not reach these guilty beings, yet the hand of God found them out, even on earth. C-, some years after the discovery of the bodies, fell from a precipice in the Winnats, and was killed on the spot; a stone fell from the hill near the place of the murder and killed B-; and in a manner which astonished those who saw it; B-r went mad and died in a most miserable state, having attempted several times to commit suicide; H– hanged himself; and A–, after lying ten weeks on his death-bed, declared that he, C–, H–, B–, and B-r, did rob, murder, and bury the gentleman and lady whom they met in the Winnats: adding that, "She was the handsomest woman he ever saw," – he died the same day.

> What can escape Thine eye, just God?
> Ah! who can fly Thy vengeful rod?

Who these unfortunate victims were, and whence they came, is not satisfactorily known: Clara was supposed to be a Scotch nobleman's daughter, and he a lowland Scotchman of lower degree; who, having met with great opposition to their union by Clara's haughty father, – resolved to fly to England, to be married at the Peak Forest, which was at that time extra parochial, and where persons were united in matrimony without the slightest inquiry whence they came. – Jewitt, in the notes to his "Wanderings of Memory," fixes the date of this direful tragedy in 1768; but, the confession of A– (published in two popular periodical works[12]) makes the date of the murder, 1758. The same author represents them as having been married on the day of the murder. This, for various reasons, I believe to be an error[13]. The author of the "Peak Scenery" thinks the whole story is fabulous – a necessary consequent of his cursory, casual, and often erroneous information. Of the truth of this tale of blood, the following corroborative proofs may be instanced:– A-'s confession, committed to paper at his death; – the finding of the bodies; – the horses without riders; – one of the saddles still (or was lately) in the possession of Mrs. Willis, Grindleford-Bridge; the recognition of the horses on their way through Stoney Middleton to Chatsworth, by the host of the Royal Oak Inn; – the testimony of the servant of the Royal Oak Inn, who was married to Mr J. Andrew, Eyam, and who died more than twenty years ago, after having a thousand times repeated the circumstance of the Gentleman and Lady calling at the Royal Oak Inn, always adding à la A– "O! she was a pretty woman!"; – the remains of the barn is still pointed

out; – and the unexceptionable, concurrent impression of the truth of the
melancholy story among the inhabitants of the Peak.

Readers, do not imagine that the barbarity of the perpetrators of
the foul deed in the Winnats is still the prevailing characteristic of the
Peakites. Thanks to the humanizing effects of mechanical genius – the
mountain-barriers of this wild district are now penetrated, and these
wonder-working excavations operate as channels of civilization! And
immortal honour to the memory of that great instrument of Providence
– John Wesley: it was the zealous influence of his first followers that first
softened the stony hearts of the hardy inhabitants of the Peak's high
mountains wild.

Wood continues to base his tale on Hanby's account, especially regarding
the fates of the murderers, though there are differences – for example, the
murderers do not remove any of the lady's clothes until she is dead (an
impractical decision but perhaps more acceptable to Victorian sensibilities).
At the same time, he makes full use of the imagery of Jewitt (1815) and the
information reported to Wright (1831). His dependence on these sources
will be detailed at the start of chapter five. One minor flaw in the narrative
structure concerns the horses: Hall fears that he and his fellows will be
caught because the horses are lingering close by the barn, but nothing is
done to drive them away – they are simply found four days later, more or
less as described in earlier accounts. This anomaly is corrected, along with
the idiosyncrasies of spelling and punctuation, in Wood (1862).

In most other respects, Wood (1843) and Wood (1862) differ in only
minor matters of style (the 1862 version also places less emphasis on Buxton,
since it was not directed at readers of the *Herald*). The main exception is
the ending. The *Buxton Herald* series ends by ascribing the 'civilisation' of
the Peak District to two main influences: modern technology (the turnpike
roads and, increasingly, the railways), and Methodism. It is striking that
Wood emphasises the influence of Methodism, which was instrumental
in the early establishment of WPM. The closing section of Wood (1862)
is longer and more elaborate and makes no mention of the turnpikes or
of Wesley. However, it still insists that the people of the Peak District had
become much more civilised, and it includes the author's expression of
surprise that the good people of Castleton were 'a little chagrined' by the
first appearance of the tale in print (see above).

The third supernatural feature found in modern variants of the tale –
the haunting of the pass by the ghosts of the murdered couple – is perhaps
suggested by Wood's phrase 'ghost-haunted pass' at the outset of the story,
and presaged in the *grand guignol* events of the second night after the
murder, an elaboration of the scene in Jewitt (1815). Informed readers of

the account would probably have seen the '*t*wo steeds, each mounted by a spectre, with hair dabbled with gore' as a Savatore Rosa painting come to life. (Indeed, the Winnats Pass during an eighteenth century thunderstorm would have looked remarkably like a Rosa canvas.) To have placed this image shortly after an explicit reference to the Baroque artist was decidedly clever.

The penultimate paragraph of the narrative reminds us that Wood's remit was to write 'historical (and descriptive) sketches'. Not only does he list a number of pieces of evidence for the historical truth of the crime, he also criticises earlier commentators, notably Rhodes (1824) – the author of 'Peak Scenery' – for their inaccuracies and their inadequate research. This is the kind of criticism that historians and other academics have always levelled at each other, from Classical times to the present day. Wood is thus reiterating his assumed academic credentials for the benefit of more educated readers, lending further verisimilitude to his account.

We shall consider his 'corroborative proofs' in a later chapter, but it is worth repeating that if Ashton's confession had indeed been written down at the time it was made, no record of it remains. In all likelihood, Wood is referring once again to the account by Hanby (1785).

5

Later Developments
of the Tale

Chapter two ended with an element-by-element comparison between Hanby (1785) and the modern online version of WPM quoted at the beginning of chapter one. Several elements in the later variant were absent from the earlier one, inviting the question: when and from what source(s) did those extra elements originate? The answer is now apparent: they are all present in Wood (1843, 1862), except perhaps the haunting of the Winnats by the victims' ghosts; and Wood derived many of them from the variants reviewed in chapter three. Since the online version is a 'typical' modern variant, this illustrates the pivotal nature of Wood's account: it amalgamated key elements from earlier accounts and influenced most subsequent ones.

Wood's sources

Hanby (1785)

Wood (1843, 1862) encapsulated almost all the elements of Hanby's *Arminian Magazine* and *Derby Mercury* articles. He relied on the original 1785 sources, not their derivatives. That is evident when his story is compared with Tregortha (1806), Hutchinson (1809) and the *Derby Mercury* article of 1829 (Appendix I); for example, he appears to have retained the name 'Cock' rather than 'Cook', in contrast to Tregortha (1806). He diverged from Hanby only in the following respects:

- The incident is dated specifically to April 1758.
- The two victims are specifically said to be travelling to Peak Forest.
- The ownership of the barn is not mentioned.
- The gentleman is not inactive: he pleads with the murderers and then fights them.

- The bodies are found ten years *after* the incident, not 'ten years ago'.

The first two points are not inconsistent with Hanby (1785); they are simply more precise (though not necessarily more accurate). The fifth point – in which Wood seems to follow Hutchinson (1809) – is entirely consistent with Hanby (1785) if the 1758 date is correct. The third point is trivial in respect of the narrative. Only the fourth point is material, and here Wood appears to follow Jewitt (1815).

Jewitt (1815)

Wood appears to have taken the following elements from Jewitt's poem and accompanying notes:

- The names of the victims (though he uses 'Allan and Clara' rather than Jewitt's 'Henry and Clara').
- The victims were young and in love.
- They had eloped because the lady's father disapproved of 'Henry' (or 'Allan').
- The gentleman pleaded with the attackers and then fought them but was overpowered.
- A storm erupted in the wake of the murders.
- The murderers were haunted by visions of the murdered couple.

It is not certain whether Wood (1843) merely altered Jewitt's names for the couple, or whether – as he implied – he obtained the names 'Allan and Clara' from a different (presumably oral) source.

Rhodes (1824)

Wood (1843, 1862) was dismissive of Rhodes – apparently insensitive to that author's motives – and implicitly denied his claim that there was an inquiry when the bodies were discovered. (His denial is probably correct.) But he may have taken one element from Rhodes (1824): the discovery of the couple's horses. He locates this discovery 'on the forest adjoining the Winnats' four days after the murders, not 'near Castleton on the morning after', as Rhodes states. 'The forest adjoining the Winnats' is a curiously anachronistic phrase, since the Peak had been disafforested in 1674 (Childs, 1987); but it is possible that local inhabitants still referred to that area as 'the forest' in 1843.

The bleak landscape above the Winnats Pass, to which Rhodes ascribed the epithet 'the forest adjoining the Winnats'.

Wright (1831)

Wood may have been acquainted with Hannah Wright, with whom he shared a deep interest in local history, so he may have drawn on her account for his 1843 and 1862 stories. Alternatively, he may have obtained information directly or indirectly from the same sources as Wright. There was certainly some such connection because the following elements in Wright (1831) also appear in Wood (1843):

- The couple stopped for a meal in Castleton, though Wood says 'breakfast' while Wright says 'as dusk was falling'.
- The barn is precisely located.
- One of the murderers joined the other four immediately before the ambush. Wright says this was Butler; Wood (1862, though not 1843) says Bradshaw, who was reluctant. In both cases, the fifth murderer was 'the blacksmith'.
- Bradshaw (Bradley) killed the lady.
- The couple's horses were found; Wright says 'in Peak Forest' – could Wood have read this as 'in the forest', thus appearing to follow Rhodes (1824)?
- The horses were taken to Chatsworth and ownership was assumed by the Lord of the Manor.
- The lady wore an expensive dress. (Wright describes it in some detail but Wood does not – perhaps reflecting the gender difference between the two authors).

- Some years later, a daughter of one of the murderers wore the dress. Wright says Butler's daughter; Wood says Cock's daughter.

It is unlikely that Wood knew the anonymous Bagshawe manuscript, because none of the elements distinctive of that source appears in his version of the story. Wood mentions that the bodies were buried in sacks, a detail previously given only in the Bagshawe manuscript, but that does not imply influence from the latter; such use of sacks was commonplace.

Elements that are new in Wood (1843)

Apart from the aforementioned 'amendments' to earlier accounts (the names of the couple, the exact date of the incident, the Peak Forest destination), Wood added elements that appear in no previous variant of the story:

- The brief halt at the Royal Oak in Stoney Middleton.
- The precognitive dream suffered by 'Clara'.
- The initial encounter with the miners at the inn in Castleton.
- The eviction of the miners from that inn.
- Ashton's remark 'I always have a beautiful lady with me ... '

As we observed earlier, the second of these elements was presumably Wood's invention, but it is consistent with the Methodist tradition in which the story was rooted. The third, fourth and fifth are probably also Wood's creations: the third and fourth lubricate the unfolding of the narrative, and the fifth reflects the haunting of the murderers by the victim(s), dramatised by Jewitt (1815). The first element, however, is substantive.

In the closing paragraphs of his account, Wood indicates that his source for that element is the erstwhile servant at the Royal Oak: 'the testimony of the servant of the Royal Oak Inn, who was married to Mr J. Andrew, Eyam, and who died more than twenty years ago, after having a thousand times repeated the circumstance of the Gentleman and Lady calling at the Royal Oak Inn, always adding à la A– "O! she was a pretty woman!"' Mrs Andrew had died before 1823 ('more than twenty years ago') but presumably not long before, otherwise Wood's phrasing would have been different; so she was probably still alive while Wood was a teenager in Eyam and beginning to collect local traditions and historical information. Presumably, therefore, he heard her oft-repeated tale from her own mouth, and no doubt it left an impression on him. Of course, she may have confused a different visitor to the Royal Oak with the female victim of the

Chantrey engraving of Stoney Middleton in the early nineteenth century. The Royal Oak was the building of which the gable is just visible on the right of the picture, in front of the smoking chimney. It ceased to be a public house around the end of the twentieth century and was converted to domestic dwellings.

Winnats Pass murders, so this is not compelling evidence for a historical basis. The apparent corroboration, 'the recognition of the horses on their way through Stoney Middleton to Chatsworth, by the host of the Royal Oak Inn,' is no real corroboration at all; once again, two different cases may have been conflated. (Wood could hardly have met the host of the Royal Oak, who must have been long deceased, so the latter titbit could only have reached him indirectly.) Nevertheless, the Stoney Middleton element has persisted in subsequent retellings of WPM along with the key elements derived from Hanby, Jewitt and Wright.

Wood may also have gleaned other details of his account from the continuing local oral tradition, to which he refers briefly in his closing paragraphs.

A Curiosity

Fourteen years after Wood's *Buxton Herald* series, the first episode of a romantic fantasy loosely based on the murder story was published in the *Monthly Penny Magazine* (Barrow, 1857)[1]. Barrow's tale seems to have little connection with other versions and it had no discernible influence on later variants. There is no evidence that it was ever completed. It is interesting because the author seems to have inverted Hanby's 'Divine judgment' message. Here, the fate of the female victim – named Ellen Duncan – is a consequence of her self-willed straying from the guidance of church and parent.

ELLEN

A STORY OF THE WINDGATES, DERBYSHIRE,

BY CHARLES BARROW – PART I.

"I looked, I listened – and the spell
Of music and of beauty fell
So radiant on my heart –
That scarcely durst I really deem
What yet I would not own a dream,
Lest, dream-like, it depart."

Truth is ever stranger than fiction – is an observation that has often been made as some astounding incident or other has startled some wild and fearful catastrophe, the offspring of unchecked passion of lawless conduct. We cannot travel far without having our attention directed to some spot, the theatre of some romance or tragedy. No part of England is more prolific in such incidents than the highlands of Derbyshire. Who has not heard of the Windgates (Winnets) of Castleton, that romantic pass into the Hope valley, where for half a mile we gradually descend from the Buxton high-road, winding along the highest peaks, into the rich and verdant amphitheatre of that lone and spacious vale, on either side jut forth large and rugged rocks looking like the ruins of some ancient castle erected on either side as defences? It would seem the very birth-place of awe, reverie, and meditation. In the sunshine of a summer's day, when we behold the beautiful green turfy carpet spangled by countless simple flowers, and cropped by the numerous sheep to be observed quietly browsing on the hill side, and when the peaceful zephyrs, no where so pregnant with sweet odours as among the hills of Derbyshire, bring health and gladness to your frame; the Windgates present a scene of quiet and pastoral beauty such an [sic] one in which can –

"Bid awhile the strife of passion cease
And woo the calms of solitude and peace,
* *[sic] the gale that passes by
Bears in its whispers mystic harmony."

But to hear the deep lessons of the Wyndgates you must descend them alone by night, when the moon flings her pale beams upon the storm whitened rocks, and there is a stillness which strikes the soul with its own littleness and the majesty and grandeur of that God upon whose works we are gazing; or, when o'er the barren moors the night wind howls,

"And the deep thunders shake the ebon throne
Of the startled night, –
The lambent lightning wild careering."

It is when clouds and darkness are round about the Wyndgates the heart is touched with awe and solemnity unutterable.

Recline with me on this grass-covered mound; do you see yonder door in the rock? it is an entrance by which the miners formerly went to their labour in Odin's[2] mine – it is now closed; sometime ago there was a hut to the left where the workmen or traveller could shelter, that hut was the scene of one of the most diabolical deeds of crime and blood that has ever shed a painful interest over a locality, – listen to me, and a half hour may be well spent in hearing this episode of passion and of crime.

In —— a rich and populous town of Yorkshire, resided Mr John Duncan. He was a native of Berwick-upon-Tweed, but when a boy had set off to seek his fortune, wisely judging that he that had nothing to lose could lose nothing, and that many a lad with nothing but a willing hand and honest heart had died worth much siller. John had at last reached —— which was his resting place, for there he attracted the notice of a wealthy corn merchant, who took him into his employ as an errand boy to the office. John's punctuality, honesty, and fidelity met with its reward, and employing his leisure hours in improving himself, by reading good authors, &c., he became qualified for advancement, and having secured the confidence of his employer, was at last taken into partnership, and became rich and respectable. John married for love, and was happy; his wife being the daughter of a poor tradesman, whose worth was her dower, and a good one it was, for a sunny smile and a comfortable hearth, with a pleasant chat always greeted him when his day's duties were over, and he and his own 'Jeanie' met to partake together, to feast over a cup of good souchong, and a loving tete-a-tete. The fruit of this marriage was one child – a daughter Ellen, in whom they concentrated all the treasures of their affection and hopes. At the early age of twelve years Ellen was deprived of the maternal solicitude of Mrs. Duncan, at an age which requires so much watchfulness and care to see that the lessons of virtue and principle become taken as the ground of action. When the mind begins to awaken to a sense of its own independence, it is then the want of a wise and prudent mother is more especially felt. Mrs Duncan had striven, notwithstanding her entire devotedness to her child, to imbue her mind early with those sentiments which are alike the ornament and defence of woman, and to store her mind with whatever could improve. Being a woman of sense, she strove not so much to load her memory, as to exercise reflection to that which was good, and to influence inclination to choose it. But this excellent system was checked by her unfortunate demise, and the lavish fondness of the father, by no means possessed of the highest perceptive faculties, by indulging his daughter in all things, gave a considerable modification to her education. Hence, while Ellen was generally clear in her own convictions of right, she was as often overcome by passion; she wanted the moral strength to overcome inclination, which, when her right feeling prevailed, overwhelmed her in regret. One thing was wanting which would have kept passion in subjection, and brought all her moral principles to bear in the hour of temptation and danger, – she was destitute of the grace of God. Though brought up to attend regularly at church, yet Ellen had never found the power of religion, which would otherwise have given firmness and stability to the many pleasing traits of her character, and erected an insurmountable barrier against the overflowings of temptation;

> "But if she wisely fear the tempest's shock,
> And seek and circle round some massive rock,
> Strong in his strength, her weakness shall abide,
> His crags shall stay her, and his clefts shall hide!
> So let the tendrils of the heart be wound
> The changeless omnipresent God around,
> Nor chance, nor death, those life strings then can tear,
> Nor treachery blight them into sere despair" H. STOWELL.

I suppose I must be orthodox, and give you a description of the heroine of my short narrative. Ellen's beauty was of a character rarely seen; it was pure Saxon, the flaxen ringlets, glittering like the last glances of the sun when his rays are chastened by the approach of night, – her full blue eyes, whose look was softness and emotion, seemed to emit only gentleness and affection, – her smile was heaven, few could resist it, – her person slightly, yet full developed, at the time of my story, when she was of the age of twenty, was such as a sculptor might have taken as a model for his choicest production. Alas! that I should have to relate so melancholy a story of so fair a being, but adherence to the facts of my narrative must be maintained, we will together shed a tear over fair Ellen's melancholy fate. The grave has now received her, – many winters have chilled the clods of her resting place. Let her folly and misfortune survive as a beacon to deter others from encountering the rock on which the bark of her happiness was wrecked.

After Wood

After 1862, no further variants were published as 'stories' or 'folktales' until well into the twentieth century. No account of the Winnats Pass murders appears in Addy (1895a, b) or in Turner (1901), though Addy – who specialised in collecting tales from oral sources, often attempting to simulate the dialect and accent of the teller – knew Peak District well and wrote, for example, an article about the celebrated Castleton Garland Day[3] (Addy, 1901). Rogerson (1901) repeated the Wolley Manuscript version and reiterated some elements of Wood's 1862 account, and he added interesting details that may relate to the historical basis of the story (see next chapter), but he did not offer us a 'new variant'. The 1883 *Derby Mercury* article about the murders (Appendix I) is interesting because the author was clearly unaware of *any* variant of the tale, including Wood's.

Paradoxically, the rise of folklore collecting in England may have marginalised WPM. Pioneers such as Sabine Baring-Gould, Edwin Hartland and Andrew Lang were interested in Wonder Tales (fairy stories, fantastic tales with apparently immemorial roots), and quasi-mythical figures such as King Arthur and Robin Hood, not in local legends dating from the fairly recent past. Also, for these nineteenth century collectors, the 'folk' were agricultural peasants, not lead miners. Moreover, following their German and Scandinavian antecedents, they were concerned with tales that belonged to wider traditions, not with purely local stories. By their standards, therefore, WPM was not strictly a 'folktale' and hence, perhaps, not worthy of collection. That point will be explored further in chapter seven.

Short Accounts in Late Nineteenth and Twentieth Century Tourist Publications and Local Histories

Concomitantly with the growth of Peak District tourism, a succession of tourist guides, travelogues and personal reminiscences of the area appeared in print, and many of them referred to the Winnats Pass murders. Thus, the precedent set by Hutchinson (1809) and Rhodes (1824) was followed. Some of these short accounts are interesting.

Black's Tourist Guide to Derbyshire (1866) adds the following sentence[4] to a description of the Winnats Pass:

This chasm was the scene, some years ago, of a most mournful tragedy – the murder of a young man and woman while on their wedding trip, which has given rise to several traditions, and been a prolific theme both for the poet and the romance writer.

Croston (1868) is slightly more discursive:

> The Winnats is not without its tale of blood. Tradition asserts that, about a century ago, a lady and gentleman, travelling on horseback, were waylaid and barbarously murdered in this mountain pass. The attendant circumstances are related by the villagers with much minuteness, though who the unfortunate victims were, and whence they came, have never been satisfactorily established. The lady is represented as having been very beautiful, and the couple were supposed to have been upon a matrimonial expedition to the neighbouring hamlet of Peak Forest.
>
> As illustrative, though by no means confirmatory of the story, it may be stated that, at the period alluded to, Peak Forest, distant about three miles from the scene of the murder, was extra-parochial, and enjoyed much the same privileges as until lately pertained to Gretna Green, for which reason it was frequently resorted to for the solemnization of runaway matches.

This passage is notable because it echoes Wood ('though who the unfortunate victims were, and whence they came, have never been satisfactorily established' is an almost verbatim quotation from Wood; see chapter four); and because, only a few years after the inhabitants of Castleton had been 'chagrined' by Wood's account, the circumstances of the crime were being 'related by the villagers with much minuteness'. Clearly, the local oral tradition remained strong. In this and other accounts of the period, the fates of the murderers and the Divine Justice theme are absent.

Hicklin and Wallis (1872) provide another example, and here the influence of Wood is immediately apparent:

> The admirers of the picturesque and the romantic will derive pleasure from traversing this notable pass, which, like many other scenes of a similar character, has its tale of terror. It is said that in the month of April, 1758, a lady and gentleman were waylaid and murdered in this ravine. Tradition states how the unfortunate couple, on their elopement from the south, were journeying on horseback from Stoney Middleton to the chapel of Peak Forest, for the celebration of the matrimonial rites, when they were plundered and assassinated by a gang of miners. Poems and romances have been written upon this tragical occurrence; and, although there is an absence of positive evidence as to the facts of the melancholy narrative, a saddle, said to have been that of the murdered lady, Clara, is

now in the Bateman Museum at Lomberdale House; it is of red morocco, with a stirrup-shoe, and was purchased from Mrs. Willis, of Grindleford Bridge, one of whose ancestors obtained it at Chatsworth, where he was a groom at the time of the murder.

Bradbury (1884) gives the first explicit statement of the third supernatural element, the haunting of the Pass by the victims' ghosts, and ascribes its source to local tradition. His account follows the examples of Hutchinson (1809) and Jewitt (1815) in declaring that the couple were returning, already married, and therefore travelling eastwards down the Winnats:

> Two runaway lovers, as rich in money as in love, returning from a matrimonial visit to the Peak Forest Parson, who, if he brought no soul to salvation, was no doubt instrumental in bringing a good many young couples to a state of repentance. They are on horseback on their happy way Hallamshire-ward⁵. In the gloomy pass of the Winnats are a band of murderers, who waylay them and still their warm hearts for ever, simply for the sake of their personal possessions ... The place is supposed to be still haunted by the victims of the tragedy. When the winter wind screams down the narrow pass on a wild night, local superstition associates the weird sound with the death-cry of the lovers, and shiveringly cowers under the bedclothes.

Cowen's account in the *History of Stoney Middleton* (Cowen, 1910) is explicitly derived from the part of Wood (1862) that relates to the couple's supposed visit to that village. The only addition is the claim that 'Clara's saddle' resided at the Royal Oak for several years:

> THE ROYAL OAK INN formerly stood in the portion at present occupied by the kitchen end [of the Stag's Head].
>
>   About the middle of April, A.D. 1758, the villagers were surprised very early in the morning by the arrival apparently in great speed of a tall young man and a fair damsel, richly attired. They dismounted, and the young man performed the office of hostler, and then went in to breakfast.
>
>   The adopted names of the visitors were "Allan" and "Clara". The hostess discovered that they were lovers intent on reaching the Peak Forest, there to tie the nuptial knot. After luncheon they remounted their horses, and were quickly out of sight. They were murdered by five miners in the Winnats, near Castleton. The saddle belonging to the horse ridden by Clara was kept for many years in the Royal Oak. It was bought at a sale of articles from the museum of the late Thomas Bateman, Middleton,

near Youlgreave, and is now to be found in the Peak Cavern Museum[6]. This is given in detail in "Tales and Traditions of the Peak".

There was formerly bull baiting and bear baiting in the Royal Oak yard, and some of the older residents remember seeing the ring about a yard or so from the corner of the present premises ...

Gilchrist (1925) offers a remarkable (and scarcely credible) personal reminiscence:

Long ago a romantic tragedy occurred here: two young eloping lovers were murdered by ruffians who hid among the rocks. I remember as a child seeing the blood-stained pillion from which they fell.

Hope Moncrieff (1927) reveals the influence of Jewitt (1815) as well as Wood (1862); this is the first account for many years to reinstitute the 'justice' theme:

Quite in keeping with the scene is the tale or legend of a young eloping couple after their wedding at the Peak Forest Chapel, which was made a local Gretna Green for hasty marriages. The course of true love seldom has run less smooth than in this story, which names its hero and heroine Henry and Clara, and makes their bodies hid in a cave, not to come to light for years after their riderless horses were found; then the edifying sequel is that the five murderers, one by one, met a violent end, the last being moved to a deathbed confession.

In Williams (1947), however, the 'retribution' theme is again absent:

In 1758 disaster befell a wealthy young couple, who had resolved to defy their parents and take the law into their own hands. On the way to Peak Forest, they stopped at an inn in Castleton, to ask the shortest road, and were overheard by five ruffians in the bar, who were so impressed by the evident wealth of the runaways that they felt a rich prize was there for the taking. The rascals hurried on ahead, and lay in wait in the gloomy Winnats Pass, and as the young couple, suspecting nothing, rode gaily by, they fell on them and murdered them.

The same is true of Andrews (1948), whose account derives primarily from Jewitt (1815) but hints at the third supernatural element:

Another eerie impression of old Castleton can be sought by going up the Winnats in moonlight, and hearing the whistle of the wind down the grim pass. The great limestone cliffs seem to tower above you in unfriendly fashion, and the bleak solitude recalls uncomfortable thoughts of Henry and Clara, the runaway lovers who were murdered there by miners in 1768. The unlucky young couple were on their way to Peak Forest, the local Gretna Green. Their bodies were dragged into a cave, and the riderless horses galloped to Sparrowpit.

Miniature accounts of this kind have continued in guidebooks, tourist leaflets and even scholarly works up to the present day. In a detailed study of the history of the Oden mine, for example, Rieuwerts (1976, p. 23) wrote:

> Contemporary with the above period is the tale of the murder in the Winnats Pass of the runaway lovers, Alan and Clara in 1758. It is well known and need not be repeated. Among the many versions of the story is one that the five murderers were miners at the Odin Mine.
>
> There are in fact many different printed versions of the story of Allan and Clara, and there is a manuscript version in the Woolley Manuscripts in the British Museum with details said to have been obtained from the death bed confession of one of the miners and written by Mr Marshall of Edale. It names the other miners involved.
>
> Of the names quoted, two, those of James (or John) Bradshaw and Francis Butler cannot be traced in the mine reckoning books but three others or men with identical surnames do appear to have worked at the mine in the 1750s and 1760s. Thomas Hall and Nicholas Cook [sic] were miners, whilst James Ashton, recorded in legend as a carter to a smelt mill on the Sheffield road, was actually a carter at the mine, working in the Cartgate level. One account of the murders states that the mine blacksmith was met by the other four on his way back to Castleton from the mine, and was more or less forcibly made to accompany them.

In Dodd and Dodd (2000, p. 150) we find:

> At that period the Winnats must have been a lonely place and, in the very year when the road was turnpiked [1758], a young couple on their way to be married clandestinely at Peak Forest were robbed and murdered in the pass and their bodies thrown into the Speedwell Mine[7].

The story, more or less in Wood's version, has therefore become 'textbook material'. Certainly it is conveyed to tourists as historical fact. Visitors to the Speedwell Cavern around the time of the Second World War were regaled with the story of the Winnats Pass murders by their guides. After their tour of the cavern they were able to buy the story from the Speedwell shop in the form of a locally-printed booklet, price sixpence[8]. This version was a more or less verbatim copy of Wood (1862).

A leaflet about the Winnats issued by the Peak National Park Information Section (1975) gives the following précis:

> There's many a legend and story about the hey-day of lead mining and even earlier, but one of the most tragic must surely be the Winnats murder of 1758. The story goes that a young runaway couple Alan and Clara, were making their way up the Winnats on the way to Peak Forest, where at that time it was possible to be married in a Gretna Green type of marriage service. In their hurry to get away from their disapproving families, the young couple rode into the Winnats as night was falling. Here a group of miners, who had heard of their route earlier in the day when they called at a nearby inn, overpowered and murdered them. All their valuables and possessions were taken, and the riderless horses were eventually found wandering near Sparrowpit. The only consolation – so the story goes – is that all five of the guilty miners met accidental or early deaths within a few years.

There are many similar accounts in such publications. This widespread dissemination and acceptance of his version of events would have gratified William Wood.

Modern Variants of the Legend

As the tourist industry became the mainstay of the Castleton economy during the twentieth century, WPM underwent resurgence and has appeared in many recent anthologies of Peak District and Derbyshire stories. A tragic romance, especially with supernatural overtones, sells well to tourists. The passage of time had denuded it of negative implications for the area; lead mining was dead; and in modern Britain, footpads are a threat in urban environments but not rural ones. The legend had become 'safe'.

It would be otiose and tedious to reproduce even a selection of these variants. An element-by-element comparison (Table 5.1) is more economical and shows the conclusion more clearly: notwithstanding various minor differences, most variants in published anthologies derive from Wood (1862). This is especially evident in Merrill (1975) and Smith (2004). Indeed, Smith (2004) explicitly cites the anonymous and undated separate publication of Wood (1862) as his source.

The elements numbered in Table 5.1 are as follows:

1.   Names of the couple.
2.   Origins of the couple.
3.   Their destination.
4.   Their motive for travelling.
5.   Date of the incident.
6.   Stay in Stoney Middleton.
7.   Precognitive dream.
8.   Stay in Castleton.
9.   Couple seen by miners at the inn in Castleton.
10.   Names of the miners.
11.   Miners evicted from inn.
12.   Miners decide to ambush couple at Winnats.
13.   A fifth miner joins the first four *en route*.
14.   Couple ambushed (e.g. dragged from horses).
15.   Couple taken to barn.
16.   Barn belonged to one of the murderers.
17.   Female victim pleads with attackers.
18.   She says male companion had only come into the country for her sake.
19.   Male victim pleads with attackers.
20.   Male victim fights attackers.
21.   Male victim killed.
22.   Female victim raped.
23.   Female victim killed.
24.   Murderers share out booty.
25.   Victims' horses driven away.
26.   Murderers return to bury the bodies.
27.   A thunderstorm breaks after the murders.
28.   Murderers are too afraid to bury the bodies first and second nights.
29.   Burial on third night.
30.   Later burial of female victim.
31.   The couple's horses are discovered.
32.   They are taken to Chatsworth.
33.   The bodies are discovered.
34.   One killer's daughter goes to church in silk dress.
35.   Cock is killed in a fall.
36.   Bradshaw is killed by rock.
37.   Hall commits suicide by hanging.
38.   Butler goes insane.
39.   Ashton buys horses but they all die.
40.   Ashton says 'I always have a beautiful lady with me.'

41. Ashton declares female victim to be 'the most handsome'.
42. Ashton confesses on death-bed.
43. The fates of the murderers.
44. The lady's saddle is displayed at Speedwell.
45. The couple's ghosts haunt the Winnats.

Table 5.1

Element	Hanby (1785)	Wood (1862)	Merrill (1975)	Rippon (1982)	Clarke (1991)	Eisenberg (1992)	Bell (1993)	Smith (2004)	Armitage (2008)
1	-	Allan and Clara	Allan and Clara	Allan and Clara	Henry and Clara	Allan and Clara	Alan and Clara/ Sarah	Allan and Clara	Alan and Clara
2	Scotland	Scotland	Scotland	Scotland	-ᵃ	Scotland	-	Clara: nobleman's daughter. Allan: southern English gentleman	Scotland
3	'Matrimonial affair'	Peak Forest	Peak Forest	Peak Forest	Peak Forest	Peak Forest	Peak Forest	Peak Forest	Peak Forest
4	-	Clara's parents against marriage	Clara's parents against marriage	Clara's father against marriageᶜ	-ᵃ	-	Clara's father against marriageᶜ	-ᵃ	Clara's father against marriageᵈ
5	c. 1758?	April 1758	April 1758	April 1758	1758	1748	-	Spring 1758	April 1758
6	-	After dawn	After dawn	+	-ᵃ	Overnight	+	+	-
7	-	+	+	+	+	+	+	+	-
8	-	+	+	+	+	+	+	+	Overnight
9	-	+	+	+	+	+	+	+	+
10	Ashton, Bradshaw, Butler, Cock, Hall	Ashton, Butler, Cock, Hall	Ashton, Butler, Cook, Hall	Ashton, Butler, Cook, Hall	-ᵃ	Ashton	Ashton, Butler, Cook, Hall	-ᵃ	Ashton, Butler, Cook, Hall
11	-	+	+	+	-ᵃ	+	+	-ᵃ	-
12	-	+	+	+	+	+	+	+	-
13	-	Bradshawᵇ	Bradshawᵇ	Bradshawᵇ	-ᵃ	-	+	+	-
14	+	+	+	Half way through Pass	+	+	+	+	+
15	+	+	+	+	+	-	+	+	-
16	+	-	+	-	-ᵃ	-	-	-ᵃ	-
17	+	+	+	+	-ᵃ	+	-	-ᵃ	-
18	+	+	-	-	-ᵃ	-	-	-ᵃ	-
19	-	+	+	+	-ᵃ	-	+	+	-

20	-	+	+	+	-a	-	+	-a	+
21	Throat cut	Throat cut	+	+	+	Pickaxes	+	Pickaxes	+
22	-	-	-	-	-a	-	-	-a	+
23	Pick	Pick	+	+	+	Pickaxes	+	Pickaxes	+
24	£200	£200	£200	£200	-a	£200	£200	£200	+
25	-	+	-	-	-a	-	Fled back to Castleton	-a	-
26	+	+	+	+	In barn	Nearby, in sack	+	+	+
27	-	+	-	-	-a	-	-	-a	-
28	+	+	+	-	-a	-	-	+	+
29	+	Engine shaft	Engine shaft, in sack;	-	-a	-	-	Near barn	4th night
30	-	-	-	-	-a	-	-	-a	-
31	-	4th day near Winnats	4th day	+	-	-	-	Near Winnats	Near Pass
32	-	+	+	-	-a	-	-	-a	-
33	10 years before report	10 years after crime	10 years after crime	Late 1760s	Many years later	-	10 years later	Many years later	10 years later
34	-	Some years later (Cock's daughter)	Shortly after murders	-	-a	-	-	+	-
35	+	+	+	+	-a	-	+	+a	'Died within a year'
36	+	+	+	+	+a	+a	+	+a	Died mysteriously in Winnats
37	+	+	+	+	+a	+a	+	+a	+
38	+	+	+	+	+a	+a	+	+a	'Butley' died mysteriously in Winnats
39	+	+	+	+	-a	-	+	+a	-
40	-	+	-	-	-a	-	-	+	-
41	+	+	-	-	-a	-	-	+	-
42	+	+	+	+	-a	+	+	+	-
43	Hand of God	Hand of God	-	Natural justice	Supernatural power	Misfortunes	-	Hand of God	Poetic justice
44	-	(-)	+	-	+	+	+	+	+
45	-	-	-	-	+	+	-	-a	+

[a] Murderers not named
[b] Joined the others under duress
[c] Clara's brother had threatened Allan's life
[d] Alan was a penniless labourer and Clara's father had threatened to shoot him.

Thus, WPM continues to grow, producing forms that are for the most parts variants of Wood (1862). Yet Hanby's original account is still discernable amid all the subsequent accretions, just as the remnants of a Norman keep – modified and degenerate – may remain as a visible part of a country house that has subsequently been overlaid with Tudor, Georgian and Victorian additions.

Online Versions

The online version quoted in full at the beginning of chapter one is not unique. Many others more or less summarise Wood's story, though most of them add the haunting of the Pass by the victims' ghosts. The following examples represent a cross-section:

http://www.the-ghosthunters.co.uk/haunted_locations_pg2.html:

> England – Derby – Winnats Pass – the story is that a couple wanted to marry the parents were against this happening. The young couple decided to elope and marry. This was in the eighteenth century so they had to go along Winnats Pass a dark steep road on foot it was the only route. It was dangerous as it was just the 2 of them well 3 lead-miners jumped on them they robbed them both and killed them. The bodies weren't found until years later. The miners were never caught for it but the story has it you can hear their cries and sometimes see them along that route.

http://www.sheffieldforum.co.uk/showthread.php?t=235866:

> There are supposed to be the ghosts of a young couple haunting Winnats Pass. I can't recall exactly, but they were either on their way to be married somewhere Buxton way (it was the Peak version of Gretna Green) or they were on their way back. They were attacked in the Pass and murdered by 4 or 5 men. Their horse's saddle was found hidden in a cave within the Pass itself.
>
> The story goes that each of the men forever suffered ill luck and died horribly.

http://www.zurichmansion.org/parks/winnats.html:

> The Winnats, in Castleton, Derbyshire, is a rocky, cavernous area, known not only for its beautiful scenery but for its two tragic ghosts as well.
>
> In the eighteenth century, Peak Forest was the place where young lovers could get married at any time of the day or night. Allan and Clara were one such couple, and totally against their parents wishes they planned to travel to Peak Forest to be married. Their journey took them through Winnats Pass, where they were set upon by five men. The attackers robbed them of their savings and then dragged them into the bushes at the roadside. The five miners then killed Allan with an axe in front of Clara, then raped her and eventually beat her to death.
>
> The next night, filled with drink, the miners came back to the spot where they had killed the young couple and put them into sacks and buried them. Since then, strange noises and the sound of anguished cries can be heard around the spot where they were murdered, and some witnesses even claim they have seen the ghosts of the young couple running in and out of the trees.
>
> Years later, miners were digging in a mine shaft nearby when they came across the skeletons of a young man and woman holding hands. They were believed to be those of the murdered couple, and to this day the ominous sounds of something being dragged along the floor and pitiful cries of help can still be heard[9].

The Peak Experience website[10] contains the following summary of Wood's story:

Ill-starred Young Lovers

> At Winnats Pass you may meet the ghosts of Allan and Clara, a young Scottish couple murdered on their way to be married. In 1758 they rode to Peak Forest to be married at the 'runaway church' but never made it. They had stopped at a local inn, and some miners spotted their wealth. The couple were robbed and murdered. Their horses were found on the fourth day, and 10 years later their bodies were found in a mineshaft. You can still see Clara's saddle.

Divine Judgement

Nobody was ever charged for the murder, but the murderers did suffer in life. James Ashton bought a few horses with his share of the money. They soon died and Ashton was so troubled that he confessed on his deathbed. Nicholas Cook was walking near the crime site when he fell and died instantly. Thomas Hall hung himself. John Bradshaw walked up the pass one day, and a stone hit him on the head and killed him near the scene of the crime. Finally, Francis Butler's memories of the murder drove him mad and he often tried to commit suicide, until he died naturally but miserable.

The Evolution of the Story

The following flow diagram summarises the evolution of the Winnats Pass murders folktale as we have traced it in this book. Aside from the putative historical basis – the actual murder of a travelling couple – we have been able to identify four important 'external' influences, which are indicated in upper-case type in the flow diagram:

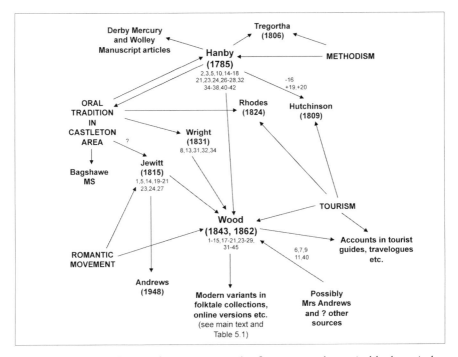

Summary of the evolution of WPM. External influences are shown in block capitals. The small numbers refer to the elements listed in Table 5.1.

- A local oral tradition, which seems to have been active from the time of the alleged murders until (probably) the 1860s, after which it may have gone into relative decline.
- The establishment of Methodism in the Peak District and elsewhere.
- The growth of the Romantic Movement, among the manifestations of which were narrative poetry, the Gothic story-writing tradition and the collection of folklore.
- The rise of the tourist industry in the Peak District, especially the Castleton area.

As the flow diagram indicates, two of the tale's many variants were pivotal in its evolution: Hanby (1785) and Wood (1843, 1862). That is why an entire chapter of this book has been devoted to each. But this summary of the folktale's history leaves two broad questions unanswered:

1. Does the available evidence allow us to infer anything about the historical event(s) upon which the story is supposedly based?
2. What exactly does 'evolution of a legend' mean in this context? More precisely: is it strictly correct to describe the WPM legend as a 'folktale', and how should we understand the word 'evolution'?

These questions will be considered in the two remaining chapters.

6

Historical Aspects

The murders in the Winnats Pass almost certainly happened, and notwithstanding their different motives for telling the story, Hanby (1785) and Wood (1843) gave us windows into the incident. What can the critical eye discern through those windows?

The Alleged Murderers

The dates of birth and death of the five men implicated in the crime could help us to pinpoint the date of the incident. Unfortunately, eighteenth century parish registers are not always decipherable and are sometimes incomplete, and there are few other sources of information. Also, personal names are notoriously mutable during oral transmission of tales. It is therefore fortunate, even surprising, that at least two of the five named culprits can be identified unequivocally. The other three are more difficult, though there are plausible identifications for two of them.

James Ashton

The Castleton parish register (DRO D1432 A/P1/1-2) gives definite details about James Ashton. He was christened on 27 March 1726, the son of Benjamin and Dorothea Ashton of that parish, and married Nicholas Cock's cousin Mary[1] at Castleton on 6 October 1743. James and Mary are recorded as having six children: Betty born 29 August 1744, James born in 1747 (the day and month are unreadable), John born 17 April 1750, William born 25 April 1753, Micah born 20 October 1756, and another Betty born 16 July 1760. As reported by Flindall (2005), James

Ashton was buried on 18 October 1778. The claim in Hanby (1785) that he had died early in December 1758 is therefore inaccurate. The entry for his burial does appear to be slightly defaced, as Rogerson (1901) states, but most of the other entries pertaining to him are clear and show no signs of interference. There is mention of the burial of 'James Ashton Widower' on 19 April 1776, but that is presumably a different James Ashton.

There is independent evidence that Ashton owned horses, as most variants of the tale allege; he is recorded as paying 10 shillings duty for a saddled horse on 12 February 1776 (Derby Local Studies Library MS 9237 052 No. 106).

Nicholas Cock

In the early eighteenth century, entries in the parish registers were Latinised, but not always reliably. DRO D1432 A/P1/1-2 tells us that William (Gulielmus), the son of Samson and Elizabeth Cock, was christened on 22 July 1730. There is no record of christening of 'Nicholas Cock', but neither does 'William Cock' appear elsewhere in the Castleton register – except as Nicholas's son (see below). The christening record is therefore almost certainly a mistranslation of the name, and may account for the insistence by Shawcross (1903) that the alleged Winnats Pass murderer was 'William Cock'.

Nicholas married Mary Barber on 2 April 1746. Five children are recorded: William born some time in 1747, Hannah born 11 August 1750, Milly born 23 April 1753, Rebecca born 1 December 1757 and Charles born 22 August 1761. However, there appears to have been another daughter, Alice, who died in 1756 (she was buried on 3 March). The Cock family seems to have been unlucky: Rebecca was drowned in the brook, presumably Peak Hole Water (Shawcross, 1903), and was buried on 14 September 1759; and Charles was buried on 6 March 1765. As we know, Nicholas himself was killed in 1766, and his burial on 29 December is duly recorded in the register. Some variants of the murder story tell us that 'Cock's daughter' went to church wearing the lady's dress, but that has been questioned; Flindall (2005) suggests that we should read 'wife' for 'daughter'. However, if (a) the daughter in question was Cock's eldest, Hannah; (b) she only went to church in the dress after the bodies had been discovered, as Wood (1843, 1862) implies; (c) the bodies were found ten years before Thomas Marshall told the story to Thomas Hanby, i.e. in 1768; then the claim is possible. Hannah would have been eighteen by then.

We know a few other facts about Nicholas. He is recorded as a miner in the reckoning books for 1761-78, but not those for 1752-61, though his father and two other men with the same surname (Jonathan and Richard) are listed (DRO D1154 G/L 4-5). He was involved in a dispute with George Bradshaw about an old mine called 'Lockarber' in 1759; he was also active in Slack Hole Mine and took possession of it, along with partners Robert Barber and Micah How, in 1763-64 (Heathcote, 2007).

Thomas Hall

The name 'Thomas Hall' was common in eighteenth century Castleton and neighbouring parishes. Boys of that name were christened in Castleton in, for example, 1706, 1712, 1723, 1724 and 1726. Any of those could be a plausible member of the murderous quintet, though the last three are more likely than the first two. A Thomas Hall married Anna Kirk on 4 May 1721; another married Maria Taylor on 13 April 1724; another married Martha Eyre on 22 October 1734; another – perhaps the most likely candidate – married Ann Bradshaw by Licence on 26 March 1755[2]; and yet another married Mary Needham at the end of 1766 or the beginning of 1767. Castleton residents named Thomas Hall were buried on 9 June 1751, 28 May 1753 and 11 December 1753, but the only other Thomas Hall burial recorded in Castleton between that date and 1778, when James Ashton died, was the infant son of the Thomas and Anna who married in 1755; he died on 20 September 1759. Flindall (2005) speculates that the suicide recorded in 1770 may have been the Hall of the murder story, but that unfortunately is likely to have been William Oldfield (Shawcross, 1903).

Interestingly, the Hope parish register (DRO D1828A/P1/1-3) records the burial at Bradwell of 'Thomas Hall of Castleton parish' on 26 June 1769. It seems reasonable to conjecture that the Thomas Hall of the story was born in Castleton in 1723-26, married Anna Bradshaw in 1755, and died in Bradwell in 1769.

Contrary to the case of Nicholas Cock, 'Thomas Hall' appears in the reckoning books for 1752-61 but not 1761-78. If the Thomas who married in 1755 moved to Bradwell soon afterwards, that could account for the apparent anomaly in the reckoning books. It may also help to explain his alleged suicide: any émigré from Castleton would be viewed askance by the natives of Bradwell (Brooksbanks, 1925), so perhaps he felt alienated in his new surroundings. Also, exposure to the increasingly frequent Methodist preaching in his adopted home might, given his presumably guilty conscience, have tipped him over the edge. By analogy: Evans (1907) describes the case of a Bradwell youth who committed suicide around 1760 because Methodist preaching had so perturbed him.

John Bradshaw

According to Rogerson (1901), John Bradshaw died on 30 August 1774. However, the deceased was described in the register as 'son of Robert and Margaret Bradshaw', suggesting that he was a child living with his parents. Further examination of the registers confirms this: he had been christened on 6 July 1770. A 'John son of Isaac and Mary Bradshaw' was buried on 7 July 1776 – again, apparently, a child. No other references to a John Bradshaw can be discerned in the Castleton parish records. Moreover, no 'John Bradshaw' is listed as a miner or mine owner in the 1752-78 reckoning books (DRO D1154 G/L 4-5).

However, several people with the same surname were christened in the 1720s and '30s, the material time for our investigation, and appear in the mine reckoning books (see references cited above). Here, we almost certainly have an example of a name changing during oral transmission of a story. If we conjecture that only the forename was mutated, not the surname, the most likely candidate for membership of the murderous quintet would seem to be George Bradshaw. He was christened on 11 January 1733, the son of Nicholas and Ellen Bradshaw, and was buried on 12 June 1774[3]. If this identification is correct, he was younger than Ashton, Cock and (presumably) Hall, but not of a different generation. The dispute between Nicholas Cock and George Bradshaw in 1759 about the mine with an apparently Scottish name (Heathcote, 2007) may add some weight to this conjecture (cf. Flindall, 2005). Also, the likeliest 'Thomas Hall' was George Bradshaw's brother-in-law (see above).

'Bradshaw' is a more probable surname for the alleged murderer than the alternative 'Bradley' given in the 1829 *Derby Mercury* (Appendix I) and in Wright (1831); the name 'Bradley' does not appear at all in the eighteenth century parish registers for Castleton or Hope, though a Daniel Bradley of Castleton is mentioned in Thomas Marshall's account book for 1775-76 (Derby Local Studies Library MS 9237 052 No. 106). A John Bradley of Peak Forest was married in 1742 (Flindall, 2005), but given the insularity of the villages at that time, it seems unlikely that a man from a different mining liberty would participate with Castleton residents in a murder.

Francis Butler

Different sources, e.g. Wright (1831), allege that Francis Butler was a blacksmith and came from Hope. However, the surname 'Butler' does not appear in the eighteenth century registers for either Castleton or Hope parishes. Could the murderer's real name have been something similar to 'Butler'? The Hope parish register (DRO D1828A/P1/1-3) tells us that Francis Barber (or Barker?) of Abney was born in June 1718, and he had a son, also Francis, born on 8 November 1740; another Francis Barber of Grindlow was born on 19 February 1739. A Francis Butcher of Bradwell was buried on 11 August 1769, but since he is described as 'Son of Christopher Butcher', he was probably a child. The parish registers for Peak Forest, Eyam and Stoney Middleton (DRO D1435 A/P1) reveal no one named 'Butler' in the eighteenth century, and no candidate with a plausibly similar name.

Of course, someone who died in a madhouse might have been buried with no mention in the register of his native parish, but one would expect his birth to have been recorded. This is almost certainly a case of name-mutation during oral transmission, but in this instance, the surname has been changed (and possibly the forename too). The chances of ever identifying this fifth murderer are therefore negligible.

James Salt

Not only is the name 'Salt' absent from the mines reckoning books for the Castleton Liberty 1752-78, it is also absent from the eighteenth century Castleton parish register. There was a Salt family in Bradwell in the 1710s and '20s (DRO D1828A/P1/1-3) but no evidence in the Hope parish register of a son called James. This name, which appears only in the anomymous Bagshawe manuscript provisionally dated to the 1830s (chapter three), seems to be misleading.

The Date of the Incident

The traditional date, 1758, has become firmly established by repetition. There are dissenting voices: Wright (1831) favours 1745; Jewitt (1815) states 1768, and a few subsequent writers have echoed him; the anonymous Bagshawe manuscript (Sheffield City Archives, Bag C/3363/11) gives 1756; Eisenberg (1992) says 1748, though that might be a misprint. But most variants say 1758, and many of them (following Wood) even state the month or at least the season. As we have seen (chapter two), the 1758 date should be viewed sceptically because the evidence for it is extremely tenuous.

The first of the murderers to die, as far as we know, was Nicholas Cock in 1766; that rules out Jewitt's date. If our tentative identification of 'John

Bradshaw' as George Bradshaw is correct, Wright's date also becomes very unlikely; George would only have been twelve years old in 1745. Also, John Eyre, the elder brother of Wright's informant William Eyre, would only have been five – too young to be apprenticed at Chatsworth. Nevertheless, we should not ignore William Eyre's (alleged) statement that the murders had happened before he was born, i.e. before 1752 (Wright, 1831). Let us therefore suppose that the true date was between 1750 and 1752. Ashton would have been 24-26 years old, Cock 20-22, Hall probably 24-29, and (George) Bradshaw 17-19, so they would all have been old enough to participate in the crime. John Eyre would have been 10-12, old enough to be apprenticed; by 1758 his brother would have been six, so he would have been unlikely to say that the murders took place 'before he was born'.

This argument relies wholly on the evidence in Wright's notebook, and because there is no corroboration it is conjectural. If it is correct, Cock lived 14-16 years after the crime, Hall (probably) 17-19 years, Bradshaw (possibly) 22-24 years and Ashton 26-28 years. Even if the murders *did* take place in 1758, these periods become, respectively, 8, 11, 16 and 20 years. In neither case can we allow Hanby's implication that the Hand of God fell swiftly on the malefactors, or – given the frequency of accidents and suicides in the area at that time – that their lives were cut unusually short. Nevertheless, they were not 'long livers', as lead miners were reputed to have been (see chapter one). Even the longest survivor, Ashton, was only 52 when he died.

The proposed date of 1750-52 is of course tentative, but it is compatible with the few known facts and is not contradicted by any credible evidence. If we accept it, then the possibility that the couple were travelling to Peak Forest is not excluded. In contrast, as argued in chapter one, the traditional 1758 date does seem to exclude that destination.

The Discovery of the Horses

We are variously told that the couple's horses, fully equipped for travel, were found on the morning after the murder 'in the neighbourhood of Castleton' (Rhodes, 1824) or 'by the road side in Peak Forest' (Wright, 1831); or on the day after the bodies were buried (i.e. four days after the murder) 'on the forest adjoining the Winnats' (Wood, 1843); or 'eventually ... wandering near Sparrowpit' (Peak National Park Information Section, 1975). The road in those days passed close to Eldon Hole. Therefore, if either Wright or Wood reported accurately, local inhabitants could reasonably have inferred that the missing couple had either fallen or been thrown into that 'bottomless pit'. Eldon Hole had long enjoyed a reputation as a place of murder (e.g. Defoe, 1724-6); though because it lies in open countryside, any nefarious deed committed there could easily have been witnessed. Nevertheless, stray horses were apparently found there and taken to Chatsworth on more than one occasion. Davies (1811) wrote:

> The occasion of their [three miners'] descent, was the discovery, sometime in the year 1767, of the two horses of a gentleman and lady without their riders near the abyss. The country people imagined (and perhaps with reason) that the latter had been robbed, murdered, and thrown into Elden Hole; and let down some miners into it in order to search for the bodies, but nothing was discovered to justify the report of the murder. About the year 1800, a similar circumstance of a man's horse without its master being discovered near Elden Hole, induced a body of miners to undertake a like expedition, but with as little success as their predecessors, and without making any additional discoveries. It is said, that some years ago, a cruel wretch confessed at the gallows, that he had robbed a traveller, and afterwards thrown him into this chasm.

If the owners of the lady's and gentleman's horses were the victims of the Winnats Pass murders, then Davies's date of 1767 is wrong; Nicholas Cock had died in 1766. Perhaps Jewitt (1815) obtained his 1768 date from a cursory reading of Davies. On the other hand, if Davies's date is correct, then a different couple had also disappeared in the area in 1767.

In any event, it is interesting that *miners* were employed to search for the bodies in Eldon Hole. Castleton miners would probably not have participated in an investigation that could have led to the hanging of their fellows. Pill (1949) may have been correct in saying that they were Peak Forest miners; the few other details about the murder in Pill's account were derived from Jewitt (1815). The following excerpt from Pill (1949) follows a discussion of Hobbes (1668), Cotton (1683), and various attempts to measure the depth of Eldon Hole:

> Half a century later, in 1768 or so the story goes, the two runaway lovers, Henry and Clara, were murdered in the Winnats Pass. And when some time later their saddled and bridled horses were found wandering nearby a number of miners from Peak Forest descended and examined the hole for the bodies of the couple, but without result.

Perhaps this descent constituted the 'enquiry' mentioned by Rhodes (1824).

Rogerson (1901) gives interesting details that may be relevant to the Winnats Pass murders. After a short description of the murder story[4] and a quotation of the Wolley Manuscript account, he writes:

> An old person, a native of Castleton, who died some years ago, told me that when she was a girl she knew well the relatives of some of the murderers, and that one woman had often shown her a ring which she averred was taken from the finger of the lady of the Winnats. A sum of money was found by two lads a few years ago under a piece of rock near the road leading from the Winnats to Chapel en le Frith, part of which is in my possession, and which, after making every enquiry, I believe to be part of the murder money, probably part of one man's share.
>
> There formerly lived in Peak Forest a family, now extinct, a member of which found the horses, which had been allowed to ramble on the open moor, saddled and bridled. He ransacked the saddle bags, finding money and jewellery. Amongst the latter was a new gold wedding ring – long after in the possession of a member of the family, who migrated from Peak Forest. This ring, undoubtedly, was for use at the wedding ceremony. This family is still spoken of by the name of "Saddle Bags and Silver Spurs". The lady's side-saddle may be seen at the house connected with the Speedwell Mine at the bottom of the Winnats pass.

The saddle alleged to be the female victim's may be seen in a glass case in the souvenir shop at the entrance to the Speedwell Cavern. It is described as 'partly in red Morocco leather, ornately hand-stitched design, provision for saddle bags, plus a stirrup-shod (for a lady to ride)'. It was clearly an expensive item. The label on the exhibit reads: 'Side-saddle upon which the young lady – who was murdered together with her lover in the Winnats, near Castleton, about the year 1758 – was riding at the time of commission of the crime. It was shortly afterwards purchased by one of the Willis family of Grindleford Bridge, from whose descendants it was purchased in January 1852'. A much older label attached to the saddle itself mentions the historical account in the 'Methodist Magazine', a reference to Hanby (1785)[5]. A forebear of Mrs Willis of Grindleford Bridge was allegedly a groom at Chatsworth, who took the saddle from the horse. It then passed into the collection of the antiquary Thomas Bateman of Middleton-by-Youlgreave before the Speedwell Cavern purchased it (Rawlinson, 1954); at some stage it allegedly resided in the Royal Oak in Stoney Middleton (Cowen, 1910). Following Wood (1843, 1862), Rawlinson (1954) recalls that the landlord of the Royal Oak is said to have recognised the murdered couple's horses while they were being led through the village on their way to Chatsworth.

If the saddle bags ransacked by Rogerson's 'former Peak Forest family' had belonged to the murdered couple, then the murderers must have been inefficient thieves. Ashton and his colleagues might have found it difficult to dispose of jewellery or a gold wedding ring in Castleton – though their womenfolk may have appreciated such gifts – but to leave money in the saddle bags would have been, one might say, criminally negligent. Thus, Rogerson's information provides further circumstantial evidence that other couples disappeared in the area during the eighteenth century. This in turn questions the association between the saddle in the Speedwell shop and the 'lady of the Winnats'.

By implication, there was more than one murder, or more than one pair of murders, in or near the Winnats Pass during the period of interest to us. Information pertaining to the different crimes could have been assimilated into the same single legend (see chapter seven).

The (Non-)Discovery of the Bodies

Almost every version of the tale tells us that the victims' bodies were discovered. Some variants make this discovery soon after the crime, others after an interval of seven or ten or 'many' years. We have already seen examples of these discrepancies. Likewise, the place of discovery differs among variants: close to the murder barn, where an engine-pit or mine shaft was being dug; in a hole in the Pass; under a lime-kiln; and so on. Wood (1843, 1862) tells us that the bodies were identified by the male's dentition, which was perfect except for one broken tooth.

On the one hand, these conflicting accounts suggest more than one 'discovery of bodies' and therefore – again – more than one murder incident. On the other, there is no contemporaneous record of any such discovery, or of any inquest, and there is no evidence that the remains were reburied in St Edmund's churchyard, as many variants aver. Possibly the bones were interred in an unmarked grave, or in the church itself[6], but that of course is speculative.

Absence of evidence cannot usually be construed as evidence of absence, but there is circumstantial support for the view that the victims' bodies were *not* discovered. Pilkington (1789) wrote:

> ... The miner informed me also, that he found on the floor [of a cavern in Chelmorton Dale] a ring, but could not devise, how it came thither, since no entrance could be discovered besides that, which had been made by himself.
> This fact, tho' it may appear extraordinary, is not singular. I was assured by another miner since that time, that when sinking a shaft near

The market square in Castleton. St Edmund's church lies behind the cottages to the right of the picture.

the west side of Peak Forest he came to a cavern, in which he found all the bones of a human body, lying at full length. He likewise said, that upon the closest examination he could not discover the entrance into the cavern. Besides this I have heard of other instances of human bodies being found by miners at various depths in the earth, particularly in the neighbourhood of Monyash and Sheldon.

It is very striking that Pilkington makes no mention of a discovery of human remains in the Castleton area. He refers to such discoveries elsewhere in the vicinity, including Peak Forest, describing the relevant locations in detail. On pp. 71-76 he writes at length about the area to the west of Castleton, particularly Eldon ('Elden') Hole, Peak Hole and the Winnats ('Winiards'), In particular, on p. 74 he observes:

In exploring the subterraneous passages and caverns, a vein of lead ore was discovered in the situation, at which we are now arrived. But the pursuit of it being interrupted by the quantity of water in its neighbourhood, to remedy this inconvenience a level was driven from the foot of the hill at the Winiards, which is now carried to the distance of more than half a mile ...

That seems to describe the opening of Speedwell.

Of course, the Winnats Pass murders had taken place within living memory of Pilkington's visit, so the inhabitants of Castleton may have been reluctant to apprise an outsider of the story. On the other hand, the people of Peak Forest might have been happy to regale him with it. Moreover, neither Hunter (1816) nor Plumptre (Ousby, 1992) mentions the discovery of the bodies. Their collective silence on the subject is loud. No such discovery is mentioned in the *Derby Mercury* over the period 1767-75, though that might not be significant; Flindall (2005), who has devoted many years to studying old newspaper articles, observes that the *Mercury* seldom reported on any event north of Matlock during the eighteenth century, another indication of the remoteness of the Peak District at that time.

If the couple were wealthy, and particularly if they were runaways, why did their families apparently institute no search for them? Rogerson (1901), refuting the claim in some variants of the story that they were returning – already married – from Peak Forest (or Gretna Green), wrote:

> The names of the murdered people were never known. Had the crime been committed on the return journey their names would have been found in this Register. Peak Forest, with its Peculiar Court and Jurisdiction, would be unknown to their friends, who never hearing of or from them would conclude that they had left the country.

That is a plausible explanation for the non-appearance of a search party. If the date of the murder were 1745-46, then there would be an obvious alternative explanation: numerous people disappeared during the Jacobite rebellion and its aftermath, and to have searched for them would in most cases have been vain. But as we have seen, such an early date is unlikely.

The Roads

The 1691 Enclosure Act (DRO Q/RP/1/267/3-4) repeatedly emphasises the importance of keeping established rights of way open and ensuring that they remained wide enough for stock movement. For instance, a 'way leading from Bradwell to Chappell' (which presumably passed through the Winnats) had to remain 22 yards in breadth. Similar ways were mentioned from 'Castleton to Peake Forest' (up Cave Dale and past Dirtlow, or 'Durtlow'), 'Loosehill to Mam Gate', and 'Mam to Hollins Cross'. One of the provisions of the Act was to *make* a road from Pindale to Tideswell, almost certainly the road that now passes Little Hucklow and through Windmill.

If the murdered couple were journeying to Peak Forest, why did they travel via the Winnats? Of the five roads out of Castleton, one led more or less directly to Peak Forest: the old 'limestone way' up Cave Dale, mentioned above. The Winnats Pass route led to Peak Forest by a more circuitous route via Sparrowpit. But even before the Winnats Pass road was turnpiked it would have been much the better road of the two and may therefore have been the route of choice[7] – if the couple were heading for Peak Forest. Certainly it would have been the appropriate route if, instead, they were northbound.

It is generally stated that the road through the Winnats was turnpiked in 1758 (Rieuwerts, 1976; Dodd and Dodd, 2000). However, according to a plaque at Mytham Gate near Bamford, the Manchester-Sheffield road via the Hope Valley was begun in 1724, and although the Sparrowpit gate section was *established* in 1758[8], the Sparrowpit-Castleton route (which included the Winnats) was not *completed* until 1762-67.

If the couple were heading for Peak Forest and if they travelled to Castleton from Stoney Middleton, as Wood (1843, 1862) claims, then they took a roundabout route. However, the direct route to Peak Forest from Stoney Middleton, which begins with the ascent of Middleton Dale, was physically dangerous before it was turnpiked in the late 1750s or early '60s (Dodd and Dodd, 2000), so the travellers may have been advised to avoid it. Their most likely alternative way to Castleton would have been along the 1691 route via Eyam, Foolow, Windmill and past Little Hucklow on to the Pindale Road, a distance of about 10 miles (see chapter four) – unlikely to have been accomplished in much less than three hours with a lady on side-saddle.

Those variants of the legend that have the couple travelling in the opposite direction (eastwards down the Winnats) might once again indicate a different murder at roughly the same time in history.

The Scene of the Ambush

Where might the murderers have trapped the victims? The field below the Winnats Pass where the murder barn is located was open country before the Speedwell Mine was sunk and would have afforded no hiding places. For the same reason, the ambush cannot have taken place nearer to Castleton. We must therefore infer that the couple were ambushed in the Pass itself, but presumably in the lower part of the Pass, as close as possible to the barn.

Two possibilities suggest themselves. One is the so-called 'suicide cave' on the north face of the Winnats near the foot of the pass (Fig. 3.1)[9]; the

The limestone way up Cave Dale, once a difficult but direct route between Castleton and Peak Forest.

Chantrey engraving of Hathersage in the early nineteenth century, illustrating the appearance of the Manchester-Sheffield turnpike road that ran through the Winnats Pass and Castleton.

The 'Windy Bend' near the foot of the Winnats Pass. Because of road widening, the rock buttress is now considerably smaller than it was when the turnpike road was first constructed.

other is the so-called Windy Bend, a few yards further up the hill. Of these, the latter seems more plausible. The suicide cave is some distance from the road, so it would have been difficult for footpads emerging from there to ambush riders successfully. At the Windy Bend, however, the road was at its narrowest, and the outcrop of rocks abutted the north edge of the road. (This is less evident nowadays because the rocks were cut back and the road widened when the oil pipeline was laid.)

A rough path led from the Oden Mine over the top of the hill and down the north side of the Winnats almost to the Windy Bend, and the murderers could have taken that route from their place of work to the crime scene. However, as suggested in chapter four, the inn at which the couple dined may have been the old Speedwell Inn (on the site now occupied by the Speedwell Cavern shop). This would have been the nearest hostelry to the Oden Mine and to the mines south of the Winnats; the killers would not have had far to travel to or from work, or to the likely site of ambush.

On the other hand, the Speedwell Inn overlooked the way to the barn, presenting an obvious problem. So the ambush must surely have taken place after dark, as Wright (1831) implied. Why then did the couple choose to travel up the Winnats at night?

The Barn

According to the 1819 survey of Castleton (DRO D911Z/P1-2), the field containing the barn, called 'Castleside', was then owned by Jonathan How, and its tenant was listed as the Duke of Devonshire. The immediately adjacent field, called 'Bottom of Treak', was owned by Benjamin Tym and tenanted by James Needham. The How (or Howe) family were landowners in the Parish and were Barmasters of Chatsworth for several generations in the late eighteenth and early nineteenth centuries[10]. Robert How had drawn up plans of the Oden Mine in 1757 and 1769 (Ford and Rieuwerts, 1976), further emphasising the family's interests in lead mining.

Ownership of this piece of land during the eighteenth century is tantalisingly elusive, but the 1691 Enclosure Act (DRO Q/RP/1/267/3-4) may provide a clue. The details in the Petition indicate that John Eyre, William Tym and Benjamin Ashton had acquired large slices of the one-time Forest territory bordering the field in question. William Tym was the father of Benjamin of that ilk, so presumably his portion included 'Bottom of Treak' (see above). Was the Benjamin Ashton of the 1691 enclosure the ancestor of James Ashton, the murderer? This Benjamin is described as 'Gent', i.e. a significant landowner, so it is hard to imagine that his son or grandson was a carrier at the Oden Mine. Nevertheless, we recall that

James Ashton's father and grandfather were both called Benjamin. Could the family wealth have been lost in the South Sea Bubble – which we know ruined the Vicar at the time, Edward Bagshawe – or perhaps in a failed mining venture? If so, then James's resentment against wealthy travellers would have had a personal dimension; another motive for robbery and murder. This reasoning makes James Ashton the most likely candidate for ownership of the murder barn.

The evidence is undoubtedly thin, but the ghoulish story about the behaviour of 'James Salt' in the anonymous Bagshawe manuscript (Sheffield City Archives, Bag C/3363/11), recounted in chapter three, may provide circumstantial support. The actions of 'Salt' (i.e. Ashton) in that account imply that he treated the barn as his own property. As we know, this variant of the murder tale bears little relationship to history, but the specific association between the barn and the murderer who confessed may be revealing.

Conclusions

Lone travellers through the Castleton area during the eighteenth century, as through the rest of Britain, were invariably at risk of accident, robbery and murder. When one particular incident achieved notoriety – as the murder of the couple in the Winnats Pass did, thanks first and foremost to Thomas Hanby – popular tradition could embellish it with details from other similar incidents. Just as planets grow by gravitational attraction of fragmentary material close to their orbits, so do folktales, including legends. When we compare variants of WPM, the confusion of information about the discovery of the horses and the discovery of the bodies indicates such 'gravitational attraction'. Almost certainly more than one murder, more than one unexplained disappearance, more than one mysterious burial and subsequent exhumation, occurred in the area around the middle of the eighteenth century. Details from some or all of those incidents have probably been assimilated into a single (though variable) legend about one vanished couple.

Nevertheless, there is quite compelling evidence that the tale has a specific historical basis. There was a strong oral tradition about the murder of the couple during the late eighteenth and nineteenth centuries, as Rhodes (1824), the anonymous Bagshawe manuscript, Wood (1843) and Croston (1868) all testify. The tale was first recounted in print by a Methodist preacher whose integrity and honesty were beyond reproach. At least two and possibly four of the named murderers can be identified. We can draw reasonable inferences about the date of the incident, and even about the ownership of the barn where the murders are said to have taken place. Whether the couple were really heading for Peak Forest, and whether the saddle in the Speedwell Cavern shop really did belong to a victim of this particular crime, are matters for speculation; but both are plausible.

Other elements in Wood's version and its numerous derivatives are more questionable. The supposed names of the murder victims are probably fanciful. We may concede that Wood's informant, Mrs Andrews, recalled a well-to-do couple visiting the Royal Oak in Stoney Middleton around the date of the Winnats Pass murders, but there is no compelling reason to suppose that they were the victims of that crime. Similarly, Wright's assertion that a couple dined in Castleton and were subsequently robbed and killed in the Winnats is probably true, but again, can we be sure that they were the same couple? A tale circulated by word of mouth, and subsequently popularised via Methodist preaching and Gothic storytelling, cannot provide unequivocal evidence of historical fact.

Nevertheless, when the oldest recorded account of the tale is examined together with the available factual information, we can fairly conclude that the alleged murders in the Winnats Pass did occur – though they were not unique.

The Winnats Pass Murder Story as an 'Evolving Legend'

Has this book truly described 'the evolution of a Peak District legend', as its subtitle claims? Specifically: in what sense is WPM a 'legend' or 'folktale', in what sense has it 'evolved', and by what mechanisms has it done so? This final chapter considers these questions in relation to folklore studies and to research on human memory.

WPM 'Legend' or 'Folktale'

The word 'folktale' is used in both broad and narrow senses. In the narrow sense, 'folktales' comprise Wonder Tales ('fairy-tales', known in the German tradition as *märchen*), animal fables, tall stories, and a few more realistic tales called 'novelles'. Legends and personal anecdotes, which claim to be true, are excluded from the category. This narrow definition was articulated in the influential classification by Aarne and Thompson (1995)[1] and has been further restricted to Wonder Tales alone by scholars such as Propp (1968), Ben-Amos (1983) and a number of American authors. Ben-Amos (1983), for example, characterises folktales as necessarily traditional (timeless, undateable), irrational (involving supernatural agencies or events), rural (rooted in an agrarian, village-centred peasantry), anonymous, communal in origin, universal in theme and orally transmitted or communicated. This restricted characterisation excludes WPM on several grounds. In particular, Ben-Amos (1983) states that 'As long as stories, songs, and proverbs conform with the principle of oral circulation and transmission, they are qualified as 'pure' folklore, but when; alas, somewhere along the line they contact written texts, they are branded 'contaminated,' since they no longer represent the primary expression of man'. However, it seems absurd to insist on such criteria in a culture that has been literate for centuries. Stories in the modern developed world grow and multiply in all available media, old and new; they pass from oral tellers into anthologies, newspapers, guidebooks, and the internet; they may return from such written sources to oral transmission. Olrik (1982) asserts: 'Written sources may contribute to oral narratives but are almost never accurately orally transmitted, mutating to something more like indigenous folklore of the transmitters.' Of course, printed sources generally show writer or editor bias, so folklorists collect and analyse oral tellings of tales in particular social contexts whenever possible, but that policy is necessarily limited to current variants. Reliance on written sources is unavoidable if we are to analyse variants from past generations and to characterise the 'evolution' of a tale such as WPM.

Most British scholars reject this narrow sense of 'folktale' and apply the label much more broadly, embracing any prose narrative that follows a traditional story-line and is (or has been) told orally. Under this interpretation, 'folktales' include Wonder Tales, fables, jokes, anecdotes and – notably – legends, including legends based on local history[2]. WPM belongs to this last category. The legitimacy of treating local/historically-based legends as folktales is established, for example, in the four-volume collection by Briggs (1971); two of the volumes comprise local legends. Also, about one-third of the folktales in the collection by Philip (1993) are legends. The genre is very widespread in Britain and collectors have no hesitation in deeming stories such as WPM to be 'folktales' (cf. Westwood, 1987; Georges and Jones, 1995; Westwood and Simpson, 2006)[3].

The characteristics held to be distinctive of 'legends' (e.g. Krapf, 1988; Tangherlini, 1990) are captured in the following quotation (Simpson, 1991):

> [A legend] centres upon some specific place, person or object which really exists or has existed within the knowledge of those telling and hearing the story. It reflects the beliefs, moral judgements and everyday preoccupations of the social group, and is in many cases ... told 'as true'. Its aim is to hand on accounts of significant events alleged to have occurred in a particular community or area and it has no truck with the 'once upon a time' and the 'never-never land'. While the fairytale is long and is told for its entertainment value, the legend is almost always brief ... it is recounted in order to inform, explain, warn or educate. Its style is sober and realistic, for though it may contain supernatural and fantastic elements, these are given maximum plausibility by being brought into close association with the physical localisation of the tale.

In other words, a legend is a short, monothematic, orally communicated narrative purporting to describe a historical incident in a specific locality, and usually encapsulating some of the beliefs and values of the community within which it is disseminated. Its historical verisimilitude is often attested by contingent detail, including surviving artefacts (Simpson, 1991, p. 28). Legends may be regarded as rumours that have attained longevity because they embody a particular cultural world-view (Allport and Postman, 1947; Tangherlini, 1990). In some cases they may overlap with oral history.

The aforementioned conflict between broad and narrow definitions of 'folktale' is indirectly relevant to this book: it arises from different strands in the history of folklore research. An overview of that history elucidates the question of how folktales, including legends such as WPM, may be said to 'evolve'.

Romantic Nationalism and Biological Metaphors

The study of folklore began in the German-speaking world during the late eighteenth and early nineteenth centuries. Its founding father was Johann Gottfried von Herder (1744-1803). Herder's pioneering work was fostered in several important ways by Johann Wolfgang von Goethe (1749-1832), whose influence on European academia was far-reaching. Both Herder and Goethe set themselves against the mechanistic outlook of the Enlightenment, establishing a philosophical position[4] that was to have repercussions in nineteenth century science and medicine, and heralding the exaltation of Nature that was to become a hallmark of Romanticism. Importantly, Herder and his followers conflated 'Nature' with 'popular culture'. That needs to be explained.

Ironically, the conflation was rooted in the French Enlightenment. Voltaire and others had portrayed the new middle classes as the champions of reason and forward thinking (which we now call 'science'), while the undifferentiated mass of the peasantry was the repository of tradition (Cocchiara, 1981; Kirshenblatt-Gimblett, 1996). According to these *philosophes*, the urban middle class man thought and acted as an individual and was cosmopolitan in outlook, while the rural peasant thought and acted as part of a collective whose perceptions were foreclosed by the boundaries of his village. Herder maintained the same contrast – but he inverted the Enlightenment values: for him, the undifferentiated mass of the peasantry, *das Volk*[5], was 'the noblest aspect of humankind' (Barnard, 1965), its tradition a wellspring of inspiration and its village parochialism a virtue. Concomitantly, he exhorted his countrymen to 'spit the green slime of the Seine out of their mouths'. He sought a distinctively German philosophy opposed to eighteenth century French intellectualism.

Crucially, Herder (and Goethe) conceived of *das Volk* as an organism (Simpson, 1921). Each individual among *das Volk* bore the same relationship to the whole national community as a single cell does to a human body. Popular culture was thus conflated not only with Nature but also with the Nation. Indeed, Herder seems to have invented the word 'nationalism' (Cocchiara, 1981). This 'superorganism' had a soul, the *Volksgeist*, and the self-appointed task of the German Romantics was to discover and describe it. Herder found it mostly in folksongs, which he described as 'Naturpoesie,' the poetry of Nature (as opposed to the poetry of Art), expressing the soul of the people.

Goethe concurred. A central theme in Goethe's multifaceted output was 'morphology'. He noted the wealth of different forms in nature, notably in the bodies of plants and in animal bones, and sought to make the variety intelligible by discovering an underlying uniformity. If all organisms belonging to the same type were arranged in the proper sequence, they would all be seen as variants of a single prototypical form. There was no hint of 'evolution' in Goethe's project, no suggestion of 'descent with modification', only a search for laws of form that would reveal the consistency of the natural world (Viëtor, 1950). Goethe extrapolated this notion of 'morphology' to almost every aspect of his environment – to clouds and rocks as well as organisms – and to folklore. He collected folksongs and stories and perceived many of them as variants of an underlying 'prototype'.

Folktale 'Morphology'

Propp (1984) adopted this same biological metaphor. His debt to Goethe was explicit; he quoted Goethe's writings at the head of each chapter of his book, and he stated (p. 25): 'It is possible to make an examination of the forms of the tale which will be as exact as the morphology of organic formations'. Although his focus was on Russian Wonder Tales, his 'folktale morphology' has been applied to other cultures. It is interesting that some of the first 18 of his 31 'narratimes' (the principal components of the Wonder Tales he collected) have approximate analogues in WPM, but whether this observation enhances our understanding of WPM as a 'folktale' is debatable: Propp espoused the narrow definition of 'folktale' that excludes WPM and other legends from the category.

Table 7.1

Propp's narratemes	Analogous elements in WPM (Wood version)
1. A member of a family leaves home (the hero is introduced)	'Allan' and 'Clara' elope
2. An interdiction is addressed to the hero ('don't go there', 'go to this place')	Precognitive dream by 'Clara'
3. The interdiction is violated (villain enters the tale)	The couple go to Castleton and are seen by the miners
4. The villain makes an attempt at reconnaissance (either villain tries to find the children/jewels etc; or intended victim questions the villain)	The miners notice the couple's wealth
5. The villain gains information about the victim	The miners deduce, or overhear, that the couple are heading for the Winnats
6. The villain attempts to deceive the victim to take possession of victim or victim's belongings (trickery; villain disguised, tries to win confidence of victim)	The miners ambush the couple
7. Victim taken in by deception, unwittingly helping the enemy	
8. Villain causes harm/injury to family member (by abduction, theft of magical agent, spoiling crops, plunders in other forms, causes a disappearance, expels someone, casts spell on someone, substitutes child etc, commits murder, imprisons/ detains someone, threatens forced marriage, provides nightly torments); Alternatively, a member of family lacks something or desires something (magical potion etc)	The villains rob and murder the couple

9. Misfortune or lack is made known, (hero is dispatched, hears call for help etc./ alternative is that victimised hero is sent away, freed from imprisonment)	The couple's horses are found and foul play is suspected
10. Seeker agrees to, or decides upon counter-action	
11. Hero leaves home	
12. Hero is tested, interrogated, attacked etc, preparing the way for his/her receiving magical agent or helper (donor)	
13. Hero reacts to actions of future donor (withstands/fails the test, frees captive, reconciles disputants, performs service, uses adversary's powers against them)	
14. Hero acquires use of a magical agent (directly transferred, located, purchased, prepared, spontaneously appears, eaten/drunk, help offered by other characters)	
15. Hero is transferred, delivered or led to whereabouts of an object of the search	
16. Hero and villain join in direct combat	'Allan' fights the murderers
17. Hero is branded (wounded/ marked, receives ring or scarf)	
18. Villain is defeated (killed in combat, defeated in contest, killed while asleep, banished)	Murderers suffer Divine retribution

Propp's 'morphological' features are synchronic in character, as observed above. To understand how 'evolutionary' ideas emerged in folklore research, we need to return to the German tradition in the generations following Herder.

Historical Linguistics and Folklore Research; The Evolutionary Metaphor

The founding fathers of historical linguistics ('comparative philology'), Jacob Grimm (1785-1863) and Franz Bopp (1791-1867), were profoundly influenced by Herder and Goethe. Their principal aim was to identify relationships among modern languages and to reconstruct the 'protolanguages' from which they had descended (Sampson, 1921), and their writings are replete with organic metaphors. Sampson (1921) cites Bopp's review of the second volume of Grimm's *German Grammar*, written in 1827, which demonstrates this 'organicism' explicitly: 'Languages must be regarded as organic bodies, formed in accordance with definite laws; bearing within themselves an internal principle of life, they develop and they gradually die out ...'

Grimm saw language as one key aspect of the *Volksgeist*, and – like Herder and Goethe – he saw folklore as another[6]. This similarity has been perceived by other writers, such as Tolkien (1939): 'the fascination of the desire to unravel the intricately knotted and ramified history of the branches on the Tree of Tales ... is closely connected with the philologists' study of the tangled skein of Language'. In the hands of Grimm and Bopp and their followers, however, not only is *das Volk* viewed as an organism, but its language and its folklore are also conceived as organisms in their own right. Language undergoes evolutionary change, and so does folklore.

Herder and his German followers did not consider that the 'repository of tradition' acted consciously or deliberately, as knowing individual agents. In their view, *das Volk* acted unknowingly. A Darwinian metaphor for the evolution of folktales therefore became seductive. However, it is misleading. Darwin's theory of biological evolution was distinguished from its predecessors, such as Lamarckism, by the influence it ascribed to the environment. Earlier ideas about 'evolution' (transformation) had presumed that the environment *causes* adaptive variations in organisms, and these variations may thereafter be inherited by their offspring. In contrast, the mature form of Darwin's theory presumes that variations arise 'spontaneously'; the environment then *selects* the best-adapted ones. This distinction between 'instruction' and 'selection' is fundamentally important.

If the repository of tradition were indeed unknowing and 'unconscious', the elements of *das Volk* incapable of creativity, then variants would probably arise 'spontaneously' (e.g. by unconscious metamorphosis in human memories) and survive only by 'selection' ('adaptation' to the cultural environment). Folktales could therefore evolve by a 'Darwinian' mechanism. However, if folktales (and language) are transmitted by conscious, knowing entities – human storytellers – who deliberately introduce changes to make them better suited ('adapted') to the needs and interests of themselves and their audiences, then variations are deliberately introduced. A 'selection'-like process may play some part in language and folktale evolution, but its role can only be minor. Thus, if we accept that the tellers of tales act knowingly, the Darwinian metaphor for folktale evolution is inappropriate. Folktales do not (primarily) 'evolve' in the sense that biological species evolve.

Metaphors are indispensable for human thought and are essential for science, but they entail the risk of what Whitehead (1925) called 'the error of misplaced concreteness': mistaking 'as if' for 'is'. In view of the work of Grimm and Bopp, it is perhaps not surprising that Darwin's theory of evolution by natural selection – initially rejected in many nations, most notoriously France – found early support among German intellectuals. However, the analogy between biological evolution and language or folktale evolution is of limited scope and should not be relied upon, lest it become an 'error of misplaced concreteness'.

According to Morpugo Davies (1987), Bopp and Grimm considered ancient or 'primitive' changes in language to be 'organic', i.e. spontaneous, and later ones to be 'inorganic'. The same distinction was applied to folktales. Thus, an 'authentic' or 'original' folktale behaved 'organically', whereas a story introduced more recently into the repository of *das Volk* was not 'authentic' and behaved 'inorganically' – i.e. as an individual artistic creation rather than an 'original folktale'. WPM was orally circulated, but its oral variants were influenced by written accounts, notably Hanby (1785) and later Wood (1862). Thus, those German folklorists who adopted the narrow definition of 'folktale' would not have regarded it as 'authentic', 'original' or 'organic', and hence not a folktale at all. In one respect, we may agree with them: its evolution has in no sense been 'Darwinian'. It has been the result of conscious, deliberate, individual story-telling.

In the last analysis, however, that is surely true of all folktales. Unless he or she recites 'parrot-fashion' from memory, the teller is inevitably a creator.

Tale Types

The Scandinavian school of folklore research developed a taxonomy of tale types on the basis Goethe's notion of morphology. Their 'types' were abstractions derived from large numbers of collected variants. These folklorists were clearly influenced by the German school; they too conceived of folktales, like languages, as 'organic' entities (cf. Harris and Taylor, 1997); they referred explicitly to the 'life' and 'life history' of a folktale, a phrase that occurs repeatedly in the writings of Aarne and Thompson (e.g. Thompson, 1946); and this 'life history' unfolded in obedience to fixed 'natural' laws, which were formulated particularly by Olrik (1965, 1992). Thanks to this approach, the Scandinavian school was able to develop a detailed taxonomy of tale types and to describe the relationships among different stories within a cultural tradition (Uther, 2004). It has been applied to English language tales by Ashliman (1987). This typology is irrelevant to WPM, and indeed to legends in general, but the accompanying notion of 'natural laws' of folktale structure and transmission is highly pertinent.

As we saw in chapter two, some of Olrik's laws apply even to the earliest recorded version of the tale (Hanby, 1785). Olrik conceived of folktale evolution in more or less strictly Darwinian terms[7], in line with the Germanic tradition, but he described his laws specifically as 'laws of thought'. How should we interpret this phrase, specifically with reference to WPM? Two complementary approaches suggest themselves: an 'ecological' approach, considering the tale in the context of its cultural environment; and a 'psychological' approach, examining the ways in which stories are remembered and recalled. Both are consistent with Olrik's work (see endnote 7).

An 'Ecological' Perspective on Folktale Evolution

Around the time of the First World War, the French ethnographer van Gennep declared that a folktale must be studied in its context, 'alive and in its environment, which is also alive' (Belmont, 1979). In other words, just as an organism functions within a particular biological environment, so a folktale 'functions' (is transmitted) within a particular cultural environment. Probably the most influential scholar to pursue this analogy was von Sydow (1948), who emphasised the social context of tales and sought a universal classification not of tale types but of genres. He believed that genres had objective existence and awaited only discovery and naming. Tradition itself is a natural entity, consisting of categories that could be discovered by scientific means. In seeking these categories, von Sydow explicitly followed his countryman Linnaeus:

> In the science of botany oicotype is a term used to denote a hereditary plant-variety adapted to a certain milieu (seashore, mountain-land, etc.) through natural selection amongst hereditarily dissimilar entities of the same species. When then in the field of traditions a widely spread tradition, such as a tale or a legend ..., forms special types through isolation inside and suitability for certain culture districts, the term oicotype can also be used in the science of ethnology and folklore ...
> (von Sydow 1948: 243 n. 15).

The notion that tales 'function' in particular 'cultural environments' is uncontentious. Folktales reflect the societies from which they originate. However, the work of Olrik and of von Sydow reifies 'folklore', treating it as an objective natural-world entity. This same hypostasis is implicit in the earlier Germanic tradition. In this context, the 'three worlds' concept of Popper (1978) is illuminating. Popper distinguished World 1 (the natural observable world) from World 2 (mental representations) and World 3 (the products of World 2, such as poems and buildings and scientific theories). Clearly, on Popper's classification, folklore does not inhabit World 1, as the Scandinavian scholars seem to have maintained. Rather, we may say that a collected folktale belongs to World 3, though during (oral) transmission it belongs to World 2. To paraphrase the analogy derived from van Gennep and von Sydow (above): just as an organism functions within a particular World 1 (biological) environment, so a folktale 'functions' (is transmitted) within a particular World 3 (cultural) environment.

The analogy between the biological and cultural worlds may be illuminating up to a point, but once again, we find an example of Whitehead's 'error of misplaced concreteness' in the Scandinavian work. Tradition is human achievement, not natural fact; World 3, not World 1. The philosophical danger, the potential error, in conflating biological ecology with human culture is self-evident. The study of folklore needs to be modelled on human activity and human agency, not on biological metaphors – no matter how illuminating those metaphors might seem.

This distinction is especially pertinent when the 'cultural environment' undergoes rapid change, as it has done throughout the history of WPM. Beginning from the dramatic transformation of Britain during the eighteenth century, the society in which this tale evolved has grown ever more sophisticated and literate. We have already seen how some variants of WPM reflect this cultural metamorphosis: the introduction of Methodism, the growth of tourism and the proliferation of guidebooks, travelogues and folktale anthologies have all influenced the legend's evolution. But this influence has been brought to bear through the minds of individual storytellers, their memories and their powers of creativity. Thus, to obtain insights into the mechanism of by which WPM has evolved – and, by implication, into the mechanism of (modern) folktale evolution in general – we need to take a 'World 2' perspective.

The Mutability of Memory

Sigmund Freud considered memories to be permanent, claiming that aspects of an individual's past seem 'inaccessible' only when there are no appropriate retrieval cues. Freud likened the psychoanalyst to an archaeologist, 'excavating' and uncovering deeper and deeper layers of memory. A surprisingly large percentage of psychologists still hold this or some similar view, apparently supported by the much-misquoted[8] studies of Penfield (1952), which showed that patients occasionally recalled remote memories when their temporal lobes were stimulated. But in truth, as most of us know from experience, memories are neither reliable nor permanent. They are dynamic, changing in response to subsequent experiences and the overlaying of related knowledge.

Bartlett (1932) demonstrated this mutability in relation to stories. He recited a story with Native American cultural assumptions, *The War of the Ghosts*, to English listeners, to whom those assumptions were alien. Later, he asked his subjects to recall as much of the tale as possible. Most of them found the task extremely difficult, even after repeated readings; they omitted chunks of the text, changed the order of events, and reinterpreted the narrative in terms more familiar to them. Bartlett proposed that unless the elements of the story fitted the listener's schemata, such elements were omitted or changed into more familiar forms by the dynamic human memory.

By 'schemata', Bartlett meant mental structures that represent some aspect of the world[9]. 'Schema' was the basic concept in his theory of learning, according to which all our knowledge is organised into elaborate networks of mental structures, which represent our understanding. Schemata are indispensable for clear memorisation and processing of information, but they bias the way in which we select and organise our knowledge and they are resistant to change. The idea of schemata has enjoyed considerable favour in more recent work – for instance in George Kelly's personal construct theory (Fransella and Bannister, 1986), and particularly in the field of cognitive psychology, which has thrown interesting light on memory for stories (see below).

Allport and Postman (1947) described a comprehensive experimental study of the oral transmission of narratives. Typically, one subject was shown a picture depicting a complex scene and was asked to describe it to another subject who could not see the picture. This second subject described the scene to a third, and so on. The subjects' descriptions were recorded at each step in the chain[10]. The authors found that the description, initially very detailed, was abbreviated to a few key points after a few transmission steps, and these key points were thereafter retained. Interestingly, some details were altered to accord with stereotypes (i.e. schemata that represent a consensus within a social group), and these too persisted. In the most frequently-cited experiment, a conversation between a white man and a black man was portrayed; the white man was holding a cut-throat razor. After the story had been transmitted through a chain of subjects, it was usually the black man who held the razor. Allport and Postman did not relate their findings to those of Bartlett, but although the two studies were quite different in design and objectives they gave compatible results. More recent studies on the spread of rumours (e.g. Dalrymple, 1978) support the conclusions of Allport and Postman (1947). Schemata play a crucial role in the perception, alteration and retention of details in a narrative, and details that are not essential to the story or compatible with a shared schema are eliminated during transmission.

Other recent studies of memory have also emphasised its mutability. The compilation edited by Schacter (1995) provides good examples. Experiments conducted by Loftus and her colleagues (Loftus and Loftus, 1980; Bernstein *et al.*, 2002) have shown that many subjects recall non-existent objects and events along with objects and events that have actually been perceived, and then insist that their misinformation is accurate. The implications for (e.g.) witness reliability during criminal trials have not escaped the notice of Loftus.

There may be sex differences in the way in which the brain processes stories. For example, a study of young children by Freeland and Scholnick (1987) found that boys tended to elaborate more on poorly structured narratives while girls were better at assimilating well-structured texts[11]. When the original data in Bartlett (1932) are re-examined in the light of this study, there seems to be some agreement: broadly, Bartlett's male subjects tended to be more 'inventive' in recalling *The War of the Ghosts* than his female ones.

Schemata and the Recall and Transmission of Stories

These studies point to the following conclusions.

• To be remembered and recalled, the theme/plot of a story must be consistent with a mental schema in the listener or reader (Bartlett). Schemata are constructed in each individual by learning and experience and are therefore strongly influenced by the cultural environment.
• During oral transmission, extraneous details are eliminated and the narrative is pared down to a minimum of the elements necessary to make it a 'story' (Allport and Postman).

Nevertheless, elements not present in the original version can be added if they are presented concurrently to the listener/reader (Loftus) or if they are necessary to adapt a culturally alien narrative to a more familiar cultural context (Bartlett).
• There may be gender differences in the perception, recall and telling of stories (Freeland and Scholnik).

These broad conclusions have been elaborated by a body of research in cognitive psychology that was reviewed and further developed in an excellent book by David Rubin (1995). Rubin agreed that to understand oral traditions, which depend on memory for their very existence, the peculiar strengths and limitations of human memory must be considered. Schemata have real psychological existence and are essential for encoding stories in the memory and for recollecting them. In addition, texts that are best adapted to mnemonic abilities and constraints will survive best in the collective memory. Rubin argued that traditional literary categories such as narrative, theme, imagery, rhythm and rhyme reflect distinct cognitive functions, each associated with specific areas in the brain[12]. He therefore portrayed the mind (or 'mind-brain') as an evolved collection of differently-functioning modules (schemata), which by working together offer a highly constrained but adaptable set of resources for memorisation. A thematic plot is necessary to hold a series of images together; the more familiar the shape of this thematic plot[13], the easier it is to retain. Discrete units in very long forms such as epics are partly built up from more or less detachable scripts (the stock scenarios for e.g. the banquets, athletic games and one-to-one combats found in most classical epics) and from the oral-formulaic phrases identified by scholars such as Parry and Lord and their successors (Foley, 1988). Shorter forms such as ballads are held together by standard meter and rhyme patterns as well as by conventionalised scenarios. Because of the power of these multiple constraints, oral texts do not have to be remembered verbatim; a competent teller 'reconstructs' them for each performance, drawing on knowledge of the tradition and its conventions. (The same body of knowledge can be drawn upon in generating a new text within the same tradition.) Conventions and genres are therefore not entirely arbitrary but reflect the innate capacities of the mind-brain, adapted to the social environment. The limited variation built into any recitation of a narrative, which by definition takes place in a social setting and enacts a social function, allows for live revision in keeping with the audience's perceived needs and responses.

Schemata and Olrik's Laws of Thought

Olrik (1965, 1992) considered his 'epic laws' common to the folktales of many different cultures. In broad terms, the discoveries of Bartlett (1932), Allport and Postman (1947), Rubin (1995) and others imply that those laws arise because folktales are typically remembered and narrated.

The Laws of Opening and Closing[14] indicate that the listener's relevant schema is engaged. Interestingly, Olrik's words aptly describe most variants of WPM:

> In thousands of legends, one finds the revenge of the dead or the punishment of the villain appended to the principal action. Often the ending takes the form of a locally established continuation of the plot: the ghost in the ruined castle ... or the like.

Of the Law of Repetition[15], Olrik wrote: 'This is necessary not only to build tension, but to fill out the body of the narrative'. Perhaps; but in the light of Rubin (1995), we might also deem it necessary to establish a 'thematic plot' – an expectation – in the listener. We have already identified a triple repetition of events even in the earliest recorded variant of WPM (see chapter two).

Olrik's Law of Two to a Scene is inevitable if confusion is to be avoided in a spoken narrative:

> The interaction of three or more characters, which is so popular in literary drama, is not allowed in folk narrative.

The Law of Contrast requires opposing characteristics in characters – paradigmatically, good versus bad – and that is clearly illustrated in WPM. Similarly, features such as single-strandedness and unity of plot are imposed by the constraints of memory, so their universality among folktales seems inevitable. They are present even in the elaborate, Gothic version of WPM due to Wood (1862). As Allport and Postman (1947) showed, extraneous details are quickly eliminated from narratives during oral transmission.

The 'concentration on a leading character' identified by Olrik is especially interesting in respect of WPM. In Hanby (1785), the leading character is the murderer who confessed, James Ashton. In Wood (1843, 1862) and almost all subsequent variants, the leading character is the male victim, 'Allan' (though our sympathies are mostly with his female companion). Thus, while the core of WPM has remained unchanged for more than 200 years, its human focus – its leading character – has shifted. There could be no clearer illustration of the cultural transition from early Methodist preoccupations during the Enlightenment era to the Romantic worldview of the Victorian period.

Story Grammars: Morphology Reborn

Any story can be regarded as a collection of elements (exemplified in Table 5.1 in the case of WPM) that are arranged into an appropriate sequence. One school of research seeks to identify the sequencing ('syntactic' or 'grammatical') rules of stories in the abstract, i.e. without reference to the actual elements constituting a particular story. The analogy with formal grammars in linguistics is not accidental; the search for 'story grammars' began in the 1970s when the structuralist ethos was at its height, and was deliberately founded on the model of structural linguistics pioneered by Chomsky (e.g. Colby, 1973). Once again, studies of language and folktales have been intimately related.

An influential attempt at a story grammar by Rumelhart (1975) used the word 'schema' in the title but 'grammar' throughout the text. This was potentially confusing[16]. Thorndyke (1977) followed Rumelhart's lead, claiming to identify an inherent plot structure independent of actual content. However, his actual analytical rules seem to belie that claim:

STORY => SETTING + THEME + PLOT + RESOLUTION
SETTING => CHARACTERS + LOCATION + TIME

It is not clear how 'theme' and 'plot' are supposed to be independent of each other, or how 'setting' and 'resolution' can be independent of either. No element in Thorndyke's analysis is unambiguous or well-defined (in contrast, say, to 'noun phrase' in a sentence). Moreover, the meaning of the '+' signs is ambiguous. If they are intended to represent sequencing then the analysis fails, because (for example) there is no consistency among stories in the order in which characters, location and time are presented.

But they may instead reflect the temporal sequence of the events actually related in the story, or they may specify causal connections. In other words, their signification is not constant[17].

Categories such as 'setting' and 'location' may be regarded as 'semantic' rather than 'syntactic'. As Johnson and Mandler (1980) observed, 'syntax' and 'semantics' are more inseparably intertwined in stories than they are in sentences. Also, categories such as 'setting', 'theme' and 'plot' are not formal symbols, as they would have to be if they were to represent purely syntactic elements; we can only define (or indeed recognise) them because they occur in something we already know to be a story.

For these and other reasons, it is easy to be sceptical about the value of 'story grammars' for our understanding of the nature and transmission of folktales:

• The absorption and retelling of a story are complex psychological processes and cannot be ascribed simply to the encoding and retrieval of formal propositions. Grammars that merely describe the mapping of a story's thematic plot on to the text downplay the story-teller's importance as an agent with plans and goals; however, stories owe their forms partly to the social setting in which they are created (Labov and Waletzky, 1967).
• Nothing in the story grammars proposed to date would prevent the generation of stories infinite in length, recursion and embedding. A human audience would be unlikely to tolerate an infinite story.
• Numerous different grammars could be proposed for any one story-line. If each of these N grammars were generalised, they would give rise to N distinct sets of rules and no two would agree on the set of all texts that could be considered 'stories'.

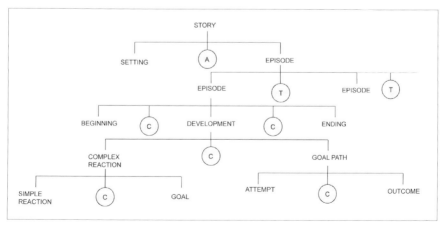

A 'story grammar' structure, adapted from Mandell (1984), p. 29. Key: A = 'and', T = 'temporal sequence', C = 'cause'.

• The story-grammar literature seems to be preoccupied with the distinction between stories and non-stories, which most humans find unproblematic[18].
• A grammatically well-formed story would lack interest; there could be no surprise value or tension in the narrative. Interest is generated by uncertainty, and uncertainty is incompatible with grammatical well-formedness.

Johnson and Mandler (1980) specified the need for a story grammar that would apply to all and only orally-communicated narratives, and Mandler (1984) offered an impressive attempt to meet that need (see Fig. 7.1). Elements in this structure may be deleted: for example, simple reactions (i.e. the feelings of the actor) and goals are easily inferred by the audience, and as Propp (1984) pointed out, there may be no specific beginning event. But Mandler (1984) showed experimentally that the structure summarised in Fig. 7.1 at least partly reflects the close relationship between grammar and schema:

- Story schemata are hierarchically organised, though the intermediate levels in Fig. 7.1 have not been explicitly confirmed by experimental results.
- Story schemata are sequentially ordered.
- Each element of a schema influences processing during both 'encoding' (the reception of a story) and recall.
- Temporally connected tales are less well recalled than causally connected ones.
- Most importantly, abstract story schemata – independent of any actual story content – demonstrably exist in everyone.

Mandler made a useful distinction between *psychological reality* of a story schema (which enables audiences to report their knowledge of story structure) and its psychological validity (enabling audiences to utilise such structural knowledge to process that particular story). She cautioned against conflating the two: 'reportable knowledge is undoubtedly linked in complex and indirect ways to the mechanisms that control processing'. She showed that schemata have a fair measure of psychological reality, because her experimental subjects made structural judgements that closely reflected the predictions of the story grammar (they agreed about the boundaries between units in a text, and the correct sequencing of elements). Psychological validity was also demonstrated experimentally: indeed, story schemata were shown to exist in dyslexic, language-impaired, learning-disabled and congenitally deaf people. Mandler went on to make the very strong (and by no means universally agreed) claim that schemata for folktales are the same in all cultures; they are human universals analogous to Chomsky's 'universal grammar'.

Mandler and others in this field have proved that all humans are endowed with mental schemata for recognising, appreciating, remembering, creating and telling stories, and that a story grammar may provide an abstract way of describing this endowment. Curiously, there seems to have been little attempt to relate this work to the 'morphological' tradition in folklore studies, which it clearly reflects and annotates[19]. That reflection and annotation is negative as well as positive, however: like the morphological work of (e.g.) Goethe and Propp and their followers, studies of story grammar tell us nothing about folktale evolution, our main concern in this book.

A grammar of orally-communicated narratives that threw light on the process of evolution would presumably have to contain 'transformational rules' for generating allowable variants. But if we consider all variants of WPM, the single folktale surveyed in this book, we can see that no imaginable set of transformational rules could generate them. A glance at Table 5.1 is enough to make the point. No conceivable story grammar could assimilate the fact that Hanby (1785), Jewitt (1815), Wright (1831) and Wood (1843) are all variants of the same legend. On present evidence, therefore, we have to conclude that 'story grammars' – despite their intrinsic interest and the excellent work of Mandell and others – are of no value for understanding how folktales evolve.

Memory and Folktale Transmission: Implications for WPM

These reservations notwithstanding, psychological studies of memory and of the transmission of oral narratives do help us to understand how some variants of WPM have arisen. Finer details may be added. For instance, because the surname 'Cook' is more generally familiar than 'Cock', the substitution has been made in many variants – even as early as Tregortha (1806). This may fairly be described as a 'schema' effect. In the adaptation of Hanby (1785) by Hutchinson (1809) the most striking change was the substitution of 'returning from Gretna Green upon a matrimonial expedition' for the original 'as is supposed, upon a matrimonial affair'. Hanby (1785) was not specific about the 'matrimonial affair', though it has commonly been interpreted as 'going to Peak Forest Chapel'. By 1809, however, 'foreign marriages' in Peak Forest had ceased and were scarcely a memory outside the immediate area, while Gretna Green was notorious throughout Britain. This is a clear example of the 'schema' effect described by Bartlett (1932) and could be predicted from the findings of Allport and Postman (1947): by 1809, most of the British population associated 'matrimonial affairs' with Gretna Green, so the association was a schema for Hutchinson. But that was not the case when Hanby wrote his *Arminian Magazine* article, or at the time of the murders.

It was argued in chapter six that information from more than one murder was probably assimilated into WPM. We find no mention of the couple's horses in any written account of WPM before Rhodes (1824), and there is evidence from Davies (1811) and Rogerson (1901) that saddled horses minus their riders had been found in the neighbourhood of the Winnats Pass on more than one occasion. In the light of Bartlett (1932) and the work of Loftus and colleagues, it is easy to see how this assimilation took place. Hanby (1785) implied that the couple entered the Pass on two horses but told us nothing about the fate of those horses. In Rhodes (1824) and Wright (1831), or in the oral tradition on which they drew, the discovery (or discoveries) of stray horses near Eldon Hole answered the unspoken question. This exemplifies the growth of folktales by the accretion of adventitious elements, and the work reviewed in the preceding sections of this chapter helps to explain the mechanism involved. It is typical of the way in which stories are processed in Popper's 'World 2'. A similar argument may apply to the various conflicting accounts of the discovery of the victims' bodies.

The new details that Wood (1843, 1862) introduced into WPM have had durable effects on the evolution of the tale. His dating of the murders not merely to 1758 but to the April of that year has been maintained as 'fact' in many recent variants, for example Merrill (1975), Rippon (1982), Smith (2004) and Armitage (2008). Even if Wood's 'April' is not actual misinformation, the persistence of this detail seems to exemplify the memory effect demonstrated experimentally by Loftus and her colleagues. Similarly, Wood's assertion that the couple were indeed making for Peak Forest has been echoed in virtually all subsequent variants. It might be true, but it is at best only implicit in Hanby (1785). Similar considerations apply to other details in Wood's version of the legend.

While this examination of the variants of WPM illustrates the value of psychological perspectives in explaining the mechanism of folktale evolution, it also reminds us of Wood's excellence as a storyteller. Absurd though his style appears to the twenty-first century eye, he achieved something remarkable. He fused a Methodist sermon, a Romantic poem, a historical account and his own discoveries – and inventions – into a single coherent narrative, and that narrative has spawned numerous offspring that remain popular today. Its features include narrative-related elements that are so widespread as to verge on cliché: elopement, lovers meeting a tragic end, villains with no redeeming qualities, punishment by apparently supernatural means, and other supernatural overtones. At the same time, it is flexible enough to be adapted easily to different places and times and presuppositions. Its popularity is not surprising. It seems destined to go on evolving for years to come.

Appendix I
Newspaper Accounts of
the Winnats Pass Murders

Several variants of the original *Arminian Magazine* article by Hanby
(1785) appeared in newspapers at various times during the following
century. They were close to Hanby's original, but there are interesting and
subtle differences among them. They are presented here in chronological
order of publication, with commentaries on the variations. The sequence
illustrates how a tale can evolve when one written version is 'copied' into
another, with no input from variants in oral circulation.

The first of these articles was written for the *Derby Mercury* by Hanby
himself, in the same month as the *Arminian Magazine* article. It is virtually
identical.

Derby Mercury 28 April 1785, p. 2 col. 1

The following melancholy Account was given me by a very worthy man,
Mr Thomas Marshall of Edal in Derbyshire, Dec. 17, 1778.

Twenty years ago, a young Gentleman and Lady came out of Scotland,
as is supposed, on a matrimonial affair. As they were travelling through
that Country, they were robbed and murdered, at a place called the
Winnets, near Castleton. Their bones were found about ten Years ago, by
some miners who were sinking an Engine-pit at the place.

One James Ashton of Castleton, who died about a fortnight ago,
and who was one of the Murderers, was most miserably afflicted and
tormented in his Conscience. He had been dying, it was thought, for ten
Weeks; but could not die till he had confessed the whole of the Affair.
But when he had done this, he died immediately.

He said, Nicholas Cock, Thomas Hall, John Bradshaw, Francis Butler,
and himself, meeting the above Gentleman and Lady in the Winnets,

pulled them off their Horses, and dragged them into a Barn belonging to one of them, and took from them two hundred Pounds. Then seizing on the young Gentleman, the young Lady (whom Ashton said was the fairest woman he ever saw) intreated them, in the most pitious Manner, not to kill him, as she was the Cause of his coming into that Country. But, notwithstanding all her intreaties, they cut his throat from ear to ear! They then seized the young Lady herself, and though she intreated them, on her Knees, to spare her Life, and turn her out naked! yet one of the Wretches drove a Miner's Pick into her Head, when she dropt down dead at his Feet. Having thus dispatched them both, they left their Bodies in the Barn, and went away with their Booty.

At Night they returned to the Barn, in order to take them away; But they were so terrified with a frightful Noise, that they durst not move them: And so it was the second Night. But the third Night, Ashton said, it was only the Devil, who would not hurt him; so they took the Bodies away, and buried them.

They then divided the money: And as Ashton was a Coal-Carrier to a Smelt-Mill, on the Sheffield-Road, he bought Horses with his Share; but they all died in a little Time. Nicholas Cock fell from a Precipice, near the Place where they had committed the Murder, and was killed. Thomas Hall hanged himself. John Bradshaw was walking near the Place where they had buried the Bodies, when a Stone fell from the Hill and killed him on the Spot, to the Astonishment of every one who knew it. Francis Butler, attempted many Times to hang himself, but was prevented; however he went mad, and died in a most miserable Manner.

Thus, though they escaped the Hand of human Justice (which seldom happens in such a Case) yet the Hand of God found them out, even in this World. How true then is it, that thou, O Lord, art about our Path, and about our Bed, and spiest all our Ways!
THOMAS HANBY

An account from the same period (Wolley Manuscript, 1778) is also essentially identical to Hanby's article, though with some omissions.

Wolley Manuscript (1788)

An account given by Mrs. Thomas MARSHALL of Edale, 17 Dec 1778, appeared in Derby News 28 Apr, of a punishment for murder ... A remarkable punishment of murder. The following account was given by Mr. Thomas Marshall, of Edal (Edale) in Derbyshire, December 17th, 1778. Twenty years ago a young gentleman and lady came out of Scotland as is supposed on a matrimonial expedition. As they were travelling through that County, they were robbed and murdered at a place called ye Winnets, near Castleton. Their bones were found about ten years ago, by some miners who were sinking an Engine pitt at ye place. One James Ashton of Castleton, who died about a fortnight ago, and who was one of the murderers, was most miserably afflicted and tormented in his conscience. He had been dying, it was thought, for ten weeks, but could not die till he had confessed the whole of the affair, but when he had done this he died immediately. He said Nicholas Cock, Thomas Hall, John Bradshaw, Frank Butler and himself meeting the above gentleman and lady in ye Winnets, pulled them off their horses and dragged them into a barn belonging to one of them, and took from them two hundred pounds. Then seizing on ye young gentleman, the young lady (who Ashton said was the fairest woman he ever saw) intreated them in ye most moving manner not to kill him, as she was the cause of his coming into that country. But, notwithstanding her intreaties, they cut his throat from ear to ear. They then seized ye young lady herself, and though she intreated them on her knees to spare her life, and turn her out naked, yet one of the wretches drove a miner's pick into her head when she dropped dead at his feet. Having thus dispatched them both they left ye bodies in ye barn and went away with their booty. At night they returned to ye barn, in order to take them away; but they were so terrified with a frightful noise, that they durst not move them; and so it was on the second night. But the third night Ashton said, it was only the Devil, who would not hurt them, so they took ye bodies away and buried them. They then divided the money and Ashton bought horses with his share, which died soon after. Nicholas Cock fell from a precipice near ye place of ye murder and was killed. Thomas Hall hanged himself. John Bradshaw was walking near ye place where ye bodies were buried, when a stone fell from ye hill and killed him on ye spot. Francis Butler went mad and died miserably.

This version seems bare and factual, shorn of Hanby's preaching, but it clearly follows Hanby in all essentials – including the title, which appears on the *Arminian Magazine* original. The Wolley Manuscript author appears to have read and paraphrased Hanby's *Derby Mercury* account. The only remarkable feature of this variant is a number of antiquated spelling conventions. Also, in the covering label for the entry in the Manuscript, the story is attributed to Mrs Marshall rather than to her husband.

Forty-four years after Hanby (1785), the following anonymous variant appeared in the *Derby Mercury*.

Derby Mercury **4 February 1829, p. 2 col. 3**

ATROCIOUS MURDERS

The following narrative of two murders committed in England in 1758, was written by a gentleman now living (1819) in Edinburgh, and who was on the spot at the time of Ashton's death, one of the murderers, who divulged the crime twenty years after its perpetration:–

December 17th, 1778,

Eye-dale, commonly called Edale, in the county of Derby.

The following melancholy account was given to Mr Hanley by Thomas Marshall and his wife:–

Twenty years ago, a young gentleman and lady came from Scotland, as supposed, upon a matrimonial scheme, and were travelling through this county, but to what place is not known: however, they were both robbed and murdered, at a place called the Winnets or Winyards, near Castleton, in the county aforesaid. Their remains were found about seven years ago, by some workmen who were sinking an engine shaft at the place.

James Ashton, of Castleton, who died about a fortnight ago, and was one of the murderers, lay miserably afflicted with illness, and tormented in his conscience. He had been dying to all appearance for ten weeks but could not before he confessed the fact. He said that himself, Nicholas Cock, Thomas Hall, John Bradley, and Francis Butler, met the above-mentioned gentleman and lady in the Winnets or Winyard aforesaid, pulled them from their horses, and dragged them to the barn, near the Winyards, stripped them of their clothes, and took from them about two hundred pounds in money. They seized the gentleman, and cut his throat. The lady intreated them on her knees only to spare his life, and begged, in all the agonies of distress, to be turned out naked; but one of the wretches took a miner's pike and drove it into her head, and she expired immediately. They left the dead bodies in the barn (which belonged to one of the villains) for three days.

When they came the first or second nights to bury them, they were so terrified with an awful noise, as they thought, that they durst not attempt to take them away; but the third night Cock said it was only the devil, and he would not hurt them, so they took the bodies away and buried them where they were found. Ashton said she was the handsomest woman he had ever seen; his share of the money, he said, never did him any good, as he was a coal carrier and bought horses with it to carry coals to a cupola upon the Sheffield road, but they all died. Before they murdered the young man the lady intreated them most piteously not to kill him, as she had been the cause of his coming into the country.

Although justice never overtook these wretches in the common way, yet it pleased God that they all came to untimely ends, except Ashton, the confessor. N. Cook fell from a precipice (near where they committed the murder) and was killed; Thomas Hall hanged himself; John Bradley was walking within a few yards of the place where the bodies were buried, and a stone fell from the hill and killed him on the spot, to the astonishment of every one that knew it. Francis Butler attempted several times to hang himself, but was prevented, at last he went mad, and died a miserable death. – Caledonian Mercury.

The 'gentleman now living (1819) in Edinburgh, and who was on the spot at the time of Ashton's death' seems mysterious at first sight. Hanby had returned to England in 1787 and died in Nottingham in 1796, and in any case was (apparently) not on the spot when Ashton died. It is unlikely that Thomas Marshall of Edale ever lived in Edinburgh. This may be a case of over-imaginative or careless newspaper reporting, a phenomenon not unknown even today. The introductory comments are obviously new, and the short sermon at the end of Hanby's account is missing (or briefly paraphrased at the beginning of the final paragraph), but those changes are incidental. The most significant differences from the 1785 and Wolley Manuscript accounts are as follows:-

1. The clause 'but to what place is not known' has been added. So the 1829 reporter did not assume that the couple were making for Peak Forest.
2. The clause 'stripped them of their clothes' has been added. That seems likely, though Hanby does not include it (except by implication); it was common practice among footpads. It is easier to remove clothes from living bodies than from dead ones if the intention is to keep the garments intact.
3. Cock, not Ashton, declared that the frightful noise was 'only the Devil'.
4. The bodies were discovered seven years after the murder, not ten.
5. John Bradshaw has become John Bradley.
6. The account is attributed to the *Caledonian Mercury*. However, a search of the *Caledonian Mercury* archives has failed to reveal any article about the Winnats Pass murders at any time during the nineteenth century.
7. Hanby's ('Hanley's', *sic*) source is now given as both Thomas Marshall and his wife.

Notably, there is no indication that the author of this article was familiar with either Hutchinson (1809) or Rhodes (1824).

More than half a century later, yet another version appeared in the *Derby Mercury*.

Derby Mercury 21 February 1883, p. 6 col. 5

THE WINYARDS, NEAR CASTLETON, IN DERBYSHIRE –
ATROCIOUS MURDERS OF TOURISTS IN 1758. – The following
account appeared in the Caledonian Mercury in the month of January,
1819. As I do not remember seeing anything of it in local history, it may
probably be new to your readers. It would be interesting to know if
the victims were ever identified, or the discovery of their remains and
confession by one of the murderers, as detailed below, corroborated by
the Derby Mercury or any other local journal of the period–:

"The subjoined narrative of two murders committed in England in 1758
was written by a gentleman now living (1819) in Edinburgh, and who
was on the spot at the time of the death of Ashton, one of the murderers,
who divulged the crime twenty years after its perpetration: –

"The following interesting narrative of two murders committed in
England in 1758, was written by a gentleman now living in Edinburgh,
and who was on the spot at the time of Ashton's death, one of the
murderers, who divulged the crime twenty years after its perpetration:–
'Eyedale, commonly called Edale, in the county of Derby, Dec. 17th, 1778.
– The following melancholy account was given to Mr Hanley by Thomas
Marshall and his wife:– Twenty years ago, a young gentleman and lady
came from Scotland, as supposed, upon a matrimonial scheme, and were
travelling through this country but to what place is not known; however,
they were both robbed and murdered at a place called the Winnets or
Winyards, near Castleton, in Derbyshire. Their remains were found
about seven years ago by some workmen who were sinking an engine
shaft at the place. James Ashton of Castleton, who died about a fortnight
ago, and was one of the murderers, lay miserably afflicted with illness,
and tormented in his conscience. He had been dying to all appearance for
ten (10) weeks but could not before he had confessed his crime. He said
that himself and Nicholas Cook, Thos. Hall, John Bradley, and Francis
Butler, met the above-mentioned gentleman and lady in the Winyards
aforesaid, pulled them from their horses, and dragged them to the barn
near the Winyards, stripped them of their clothes, and took from them
above two hundred pounds in money. They seized the gentleman and cut
his throat. The lady entreated them on her knees only to spare his life,

and begged in all the agonies of distress to be turned out naked as she was, but one of the fiends took a miner's pike and drove it into her head and she immediately expired. They left the dead bodies in the barn for three days. When they came the first or second night to bury them they were so terrified with an awful voice they heard, or thought so, that they durst not attempt to take them away. But the third night Cock said it was only the devil, and he would not hurt them, so they took the bodies away and buried them where they were found. Ashton said she was the handsomest woman he had ever seen. His share of the money never did him any good, as he was a coal carrier and bought horses with it to carry coals to a cupola upon the Sheffield road, but they all died. Before they murdered the young man the lady entreated them most piteously not to kill him as she had been the cause of his coming into this country.

Although justice never overtook these wretches in the common way yet it pleased God that they all came to untimely ends except Ashton, the confessor. Cook fell from a precipice near the scene of the murder and was killed. Hall hanged himself. Bradley was walking within a few yards of the place where the bodies were buried and a stone fell from the hill and killed him on the spot to the astonishment of every one that knew it. Francis Butler attempted several times to hang himself, but was prevented, at last he went mad, and died a miserable death."
NEMESIS

'Nemesis' has more or less copied the 1829 article with only trivial changes (Nicholas Cock has become Nicholas Cook, for example), but the introductory paragraph is interesting. He seems unaware of the versions of the story produced by Jewitt, Rhodes, Wright, Wood and Barrow, or of Hanby's original articles in 1785, or of the Wolley manuscript; except that the date of the murders is now firmly stated as 1758. As already noted, the *Caledonian Mercury* article of 1819 does not appear to exist.

Interestingly, I have been able to find no reply to 'Nemesis' in any issue of the *Derby Mercury* over the succeeding year. One might have expected an editor of the *Buxton Herald* to have set him right, in view of the prominence that he or his predecessor had given to Wood's account in 1843. At least one might have expected a letter from a reader who was familiar with one or more of the accounts of the Winnats Pass murders that were by then well known to a fairly wide audience. This absence of response may indicate that the story had – temporarily – ceased to excite public interest.

Appendix II
The Diary of Edward Bagshawe
(1690-1769)

Edward Bagshawe was given the living of Castleton by the bishop in 1723, after he had lost his fortune in the South Sea Bubble, and he retained it until his death in 1769. His diary or commonplace book consists mostly of household accounts but it gives other information besides; it covers the years 1715-51. Although it contains nothing directly relevant to the story of the Winnats Pass murders, it provides interesting background about the everyday affairs of a Vicar of Castleton at the time of the incident, giving a window into the life of the village in the eighteenth century. The original document is in the Sheffield City Archives (Bag C/315).

Some pages are missing from the diary: four single leaves have been torn out in the years 1748-50; perhaps more significantly, 22 successive leaves are missing between November 1743 and April 1747. No one knows who caused this disfigurement, or when; but if the murders had taken place c. 1745 and Bagshawe had written something about them, the reference is irretrievably lost. Nor do we know his opinion of the Jacobite rising, if any; as we have observed, the Peak District was not affected by the Jacobite army or its Hanoverian opponents.

This Appendix comprises a few excerpts from the later parts of the diary (1742-50); see Cox (1880) and Shawcross (1903) for other excerpts and discussion. The first selection, for May 1742, illustrates the somewhat haphazard nature of the document. Income and expenditure are mingled in the same column; amounts are entered inconsistently, and sometimes not at all; and the accounts are interspersed with brief notes about the daily doings of the vicar and his family. However, we can see what kinds of goods and services were purchased at the time, and at what costs, and the largely self-sufficient nature of eighteenth century Castleton is evident. (Coal was probably imported from as far afield as Chapel-en-le-Frith, where the mines supplied lead smelters in the area as well as such households as could afford fuel.)

May 1742		£:	sh:	D:
1st	Pd for 3 pound of Butter:		1:	3:
	Pd for a Hindquarter of Veal:		2:	
	G: my Sister to lay out at the Fair:		2:	6:
	Pd for two pound of Fish: __			8:
2:	I received a letter from Peggy:-			
4th:	G: Ellis Hall of Gooshill when he went to Chesterfield to meet my Daughter:	oo:	4:	o:
	Pd Joshua Knowles for shoes making & mending to this day & for shaving to Lady day last year:	3:	10:	
	Due to me from him: _ _ _		2:	10:
5h:	Pd for a pound of Sugar	oo:	oo:	6:
6:	Pd Ellis Hall for a Load of Coal:	oo:	1:	o:
13th:	Pd Mr Needham for Turbot	oo:	oo:	11:
15:	Pd Isaac Dakyn for a Load of Coal:		1:	
May 1742		£:	sh:	D:
20:	This day Peggy set out for Dr Poching at Burton near Loughborough in Leicestershire; G: my daughter when she went away: Ellis Hall of Gooshill went along wth her:	1:	o:	o:
	Borrowed of Mr Needham twenty shillings:			
21:	Received of Robert Hall his wedding dues:	oo:	5:	o:

	P^d Robert Hall for coals & leading Muck	oo:	2:	6:
23rd:	Ellis Hall of Gooshill returned from Burton to Castleton where he left my Daughter on ye 21st instant safe & in good Health. D: G: I preached at Eyam for Mr Seward Rector and staid there ye whole day. Mr Wormald supplying my place at Castleton in the afternoon. _ _ _			
28th:	Received of Robert Barber of ye Vicarage five shillings no^t remained due for Home rent for ye Year 1741:	oo:	5:	o:

In July of the same year, we have an indication of the vicar's income from tithes (tyths)[1]. He and an important local landowner, the then-current head of the Bagshaw family (no relation, as the absence of the final 'e' shows), received some portion in cash or kind of all agricultural produce and of the lead ore mined within the liberty. Receipt of the tithes evidently enabled Bagshawe to settle some outstanding debts of his own.

July 1742		£:	sh:	D:
8:	Mr Bagshaw & I received for Tyth Oar & Tyth Wool and Lamb:-			
	Received in Cash for Tyth Oar: 3^d part	1:	16:	8:
	Received in Cash for Tyth Wool:	3:	14:	8:
	Received of Mr Needham re for Tyth	3:	16:	10:
	Received of Mr Bagshaw for Easter Dues:	oo:	10:	6:
	Rec^d of Mr Bagshaw a Modus for Tyth Hay:	oo:	4:	4:

		£:	sh:	D:
	P^d Iⁿ Barber for gathering ye Tyth Oar in 1740: The whole Wool to be divided was 13: stone seven pound: my 3^d part is 4 stone seven pound	1:	13:	4:
10th:	P^d Enoch Darwent two Guineas on account of John Baddely Malster due ye 7th day of April last year.	2:	2:	0:
	P^d Enoch Darwent for ye carriage of half a Load of Malt & grinding it: ac:	00:	1:	0:
12th	P^d Abraham Dakyn w^h I owed him for Coals:	2:	7:	0:
	P^d him for exchange of ye Land:	00:	1:	0:
	Rec^d of Abraham Dakyn for a Quarter of black Oats:	00:	11:	0:
	Rec^d of him for 4 Tyth Lambs wch I sold him June 11th:	0:	10:	0:
	Rec^d of him for 4 stone and a half of wool:	1:	7:	00:

The next selection shows further household expenditures, including the cost of obtaining news at that time.

Nov 1743		£:	sh:	D:
5th	3 pounds of butter from Mr Knowles	00:	1:	
18th	3 pounds of butter from Mr Knowls		1:	
24	13 pd & a half of Cheese from Mr Knowls			
26	3 pounds of butter from John Knowls	00:	1:	0:

	(Etcetera...)			
Novber 17th	Pd Nanny Eyre Widow twelve shillings and tenpence in full of her Bill for Grocery		12:	10:
	G: Tho: Hall when he brought me a Pig from Mr Bagshaw:	00:	00:	6:
18	Pd Mr Hanby by Mr Needham eight Shilling for [...?] news due ye 17th of September last	00:	8:	0:

There were also various dues and taxes, and the requirements of court duties. These are illustrated in the following excerpt from 1747, immediately following the 22 missing leaves from the diary. This excerpt also shows purchases that may be surprising to twenty-first century eyes.

April 1747		£:	sh:	
1:	Pd Robert Hall in part for the Land Tax:		9:	
29:	Pd for a letter from Hal 8d:			
May 1:	Pd Mrs Shot 5sh by my Sisters:			
2d	I sent by Mr Robert Waterhouse a = Letter to Hal, and 3 Books: Readings Life of [...?] 2 volumes: Nelson on the Sacrament			
3d	Sent Mr Swain by Benjamin Kirk Parsons' Christian Directory. The Apparitor came to give me notice of the Probate Court at Chesterfield for the 21 instant:			
4th	Pd Robert Hall in part for Land Tax and Window money: remains due to him 3sh & 8d	00:	9:	
6	Pd Nal. Greaves for 12 pound of Raisons	00:	4:	00:

8th	P[d] Sam Slater for 2 pecks of Cowslips: 1[sh] Sent by him a Letter to Peggy			

Meat consumption in Bagshawe's household is interesting; so are the local meat prices in the years following the Jacobite rising. Bagshawe's spelling was sometimes as wayward as his account-keeping, witness 'peice' for 'piece'.

	A Bill for meat Begun with Henry Bridbury in May 1749		sh:	D:
May 20	a Breast of Veal & forequarters of Lamb =	oo:	2:	2:
27	a Forequarter of Lamb:	oo:	1:	4:
31	a Forequarter of Lamb:	oo:	1:	9:
June 3rd	a shoulder & breast of Mutton:	oo:	2:	6:
	(Etcetera…)			
August 26:	a Loyn & Forequarter of Lamb:		2:	1½:
31:	a shoulder of Mutton:		1:	3:
Sept. 2[d]:	a peice of Beef of 4[lb] & a half:	oo:	oo:	9:
6	Tea 1[sh] & 6[d] X			
9	a shoulder and neck of Mutton and Tongue:		2	4½:

Finally, here is a Rental for the year 1750. There is a similar list for 1751, which is almost the last entry in the document.

		Payable		£	S	D
In^s Mallison	a farm	Mich^s & L. day	Value	3	3	6
Thos Wells Widow	a farm	Lady day	value	oo	8	6
Robert/Widow Nall	a farm	Lady day	value	-	9	-
Widow Daniel	a farm	Mich^s & L. day	value	-	14	-
Thos. Nowel	a farm	Mich^s & L. day	value	1	1	-
Benj^m. Hall	a farm	Mich^s & L. day	value	1	5	-
Harry Bradbury	a farm	Mich^s & L. day	value	3	-	-
W^m. Mallison	a farm	Mich^s & L. day	value	1	3	-
In^s. Staveley	a farm	Lady day	value	-	10	-
Michael Marshall	a farm	Mich^s & L. day	value	-	14	2
Robert Hall	a farm	Mich^s & L. day	Value	1	12	6
In^s. Pickford chap.	a farm	Mich^s & L. day	value	14	-	-
Robt. Walher $^{Mr\ Bray}$	a farm	Mich^s & L. day	value	2	-	-
~~Rich~~ John Bagshaw	a farm	Mich^s & L. day	value	3	-	-

Endnotes

Chapter One

1. http://bygonederbyshire.co.uk/articles/Castleton:_Winnat's_Pass,_ The_Ghosts_of_Allan_and_Clara
2. The barn in which the couple were supposedly killed is at the entrance to the Pass, at the Castleton end, not half way along.
3. Hobbes's *De Mirabilibis Pecci* was apparently written as early as 1636, but was not published in London until some 30 years later.
4. Here and elsewhere in this book, DRO = Derbyshire Record Office.
5. Peter Harrison kindly lent a copy of this book to me. At the time of reading (November 2008) it remained a 'work in progress'; Peter had begun writing it in 2004.
6. She was born in Wiltshire in 1662, the daughter of Parliamentarian colonel, and died in London in 1741. Her visit to Derbyshire was included in a seven-week journey of some 685 miles that she undertook in 1697, riding sidesaddle and accompanied by her two cousins, Susannah and Mary Filmer, together with a servant and a dog. Her descriptions are historically important because they have no contemporaneous peer. Her original journal is preserved at Broughton Castle in Oxfordshire.
7. A *dish* was a measure equivalent (depending on the area) to 14 or 15 pints. Nine dishes constituted a *load*, and twelve loads constituted a *fother*, about 22 cwt. The wooden bowl in which the dish was measured was called a *miner's standard*. Today, a hostelry on the outskirts of Winster, once an important lead mining centre, is called the 'Miner's Standard'.
8. For example, Shawcross (1903) cites 'William Nall drowned in ye mine 1752... Rebecca Cock drowned 1759... Joseph Flinders

unfortunately killed by ye wheel of a cart running over him 1762 ... William Oldfield destroyed himself by hanging in ye poor house 1770 ... John Hall suicide 1794'. Rieuwerts (1976) notes: 'May 1760, Dr Harrison paid 1 guinea for setting Robert Nall leg and Jos Rowbotham arm, both broken in the mine'.

9.   Galena, or lead sulphide. The smelting process generated sulphurous fumes.

10. Miners throughout the area wore leather hats that were mostly manufactured in Bradwell – 'Bradda Beavers'. A 'Bradda Beaver' was fashioned like a military helmet and is said to have been the forerunner of the tin hat. It was designed to hold a candle to light the way into the mine. Bradda Beavers became popular both within and beyond Derbyshire and were used for other purposes besides lead mining.

11. The name 'Odin', otherwise 'Oden', is usually supposed to refer to the Norse god of that name, indicating that the mine was worked as early as the time of the Danelaw, which included Derbyshire. Indeed, the mine may be older than that. However, there is an alternative view that 'Oden' is a corruption of 'Owd 'un' = 'old one', again connoting venerability.

12. There are several claims that the Oden is haunted by the ghost(s) of one or more of the Winnats Pass murderers. Nowadays, the mine is entered only by speleologists, some of whom ascribe an unpleasantly sinister atmosphere to it (e.g. Smith, 2004).

13. A *scrin* is a short, usually thin, more or less vertical vein of ore often branching from a major vein. A *Liberty* was the district in which a miner searched for ore. Different liberties had slightly different laws and customs.

14. In her description of Derbyshire, Celia Fiennes distinguishes 'sparr' from 'azurine sparr' which was almost certainly blue john. In other sources it is called 'Derbyshire spar' (also, confusingly, a name used for alabaster). Blue john was known to the local miners as 'Derby drop'. The name 'blue john', introduced c. 1770, probably comes from the description 'bleu jaune' used by the French workers who were adept in exploiting it for ornamental purposes; blue and yellow are usually the predominant colours.

15. Similarly, a gentleman named Cole was lent a journal of 1775 by his brother-in-law, Alderman Bentham of Cambridge, written by Bentham's clerk Mr Whaley, which contains: *Oct. 11. We came from Buxton over a most bleak country to Eldon Hole which a vast Cavity betwixt the rocks & said to be about 800 yards deep – Two Miles from there we came to the celebrated Wonder of the Peak, the Devils*

Arse; the entrance of which is most horridly magnificent but we could not scrutinize all the dreadful Curiosities of this Place, being stopped at about 200 yards after our Entrance, by a River, which the late Rains had made impassable – Below these dismal mountains is a Town called Castleton & a very fine vale called Hope Vale... (Sheffield Archives, Bag C/3363/11).

16. The population in 1801 was recorded as 843. It is now (first decade of the twenty-first century) between 700 and 800. In the heyday of lead mining, during the first half of the eighteenth century, it is believed to have been around 2000.

17. On pp. 95-110 he describes the operation of the cupola furnace in lead smelting. The cupola was introduced into Derbyshire early in the eighteenth century and had more or less replaced the older and less efficient hearth furnace by the middle of the century. At the time of interest for this book, there was a cupola close to Castleton on the Sheffield (i.e. Pindale) road and another, also east of the village, at what is now Marsh Farm, where there is still sufficient lead in the soil to be toxic to cattle. The next nearest was at Bradwell. Peter Harrison believes that the Pindale road cupola was used for lime burning rather than lead smelting.

18. Probably the hamlet now called 'Old Dam' near Peak Forest. However, the name was also occasionally applied to Chapel-en-le-Frith.

19. Composition of this work seems to have begun in 1818 and to have been completed in 1823. This was the era of the early Romantic poets in England and on the Continent.

20. Citation 26 Geo. II. c. 33. See http://en.wikipedia.org/wiki/Marriage_Act_1753. Mary Williamson of Dove Holes told me that after this Act became law, at least one party in the marriage was required to be resident in Peak Forest for a minimum of one week. The marriage registers confirm that arrangements became much more formal from 1754 onwards, with (for example) a requirement for two witnesses.

21. See http://www.archive.org/stream/norfolkstreetwesooseed/norfolkstreetwesooseed_djvu.txt. The Peak District remained part of the Sheffield Circuit until 1806, when the Chesterfield Circuit was instituted. The villages now belong to the Peak Circuit.

22. Bagshawe had accepted the Presbyterianism of the Commonwealth period and did not change or recant his views after the Restoration of 1660. During the troubles of 1745, a crowd of religious opponents from other villages wrecked the Bradwell chapel (Evans, 1907); it was subsequently rebuilt.

23. According to Evans (1907), the minister was William Green of Rotherham and the date was 1760. According to Ogle (1998), the

visiting minister was Matthew Mayer of Stockport and the date was
1765. The two accounts agree in most other particulars. Possibly
there were two visits, both attended with disruption.

24. Olsen's book is informative and easy to read, though in many ways
simplistic. She treats the eighteenth century 'homogeneously', failing
to convey how dramatically society and landscape were transformed
as the century progressed, not least as a result of enclosures and
turnpiking (cp. Bogart, 2004). However, her clear summary accounts
of taxation and of crime and punishment provide a useful background
for this investigation.

25. Prior to the 1832 Reform Act, Derbyshire was a single parliamentary
constituency represented by two MPs, one of whom was always a
Cavendish representative closely related to the Duke of Devonshire
(and invariably a Whig). The Marquis of Hartington was the MP
in 1741-51, Lord Frederick Cavendish 1751-54, and Lord George
Augustus Cavendish 1754-94. Presumably the robbers would have
had to appeal via the Howe family (the local barmasters and landowners) to the MP, and their chances of a sympathetic hearing would
have been slight.

Chapter Two

1. It became the *Methodist Magazine* in 1798 and the *Wesleyan
Methodist Magazine* in 1822. The name 'Arminian' was derived from
the Dutch theologian Jacobus Arminius (1560-1609), who opposed
the Reformed Church's Calvinist stance on strict predestination
and preached salvation through God's grace. John Wesley explicitly
followed Arminius in this matter, hence the conflicts between the
early Methodists and Puritans with Calvinist inclinations, including
Wesley's erstwhile colleagues Whitefield and Harris. He launched the
Arminian Magazine as a doctrinal weapon against any teaching that
was contrary to his fundamental belief that '*God willeth all men to
be saved and to come to a knowledge of the truth*'. The Methodist
Arminian Magazine of 1778-98 should not be confused with the
Arminian Magazine of 1822-28, which was superseded by *The Bible
Christian Magazine*.

2. http://www.rewlach.org.uk/Leek100/LkC1.rtf

3. http://www.ashbourne-town.com/history/buildings/zion/zion.html;
http://ashbourne-methodist-church.supanet.com/Methodism%20in
%20Ashbourne.html

4. http://www.rewlach.org.uk/Leek100/LkC1.rtf

5. In 1785, he was ordained ('set apart') by John Wesley for ministry in Scotland along with his close friends John Pawson and Joseph Taylor. Pawson was President of the Conference in 1793, the year before Hanby.

6. This book is replete with tales of supernatural punishments, visitations from deceased victims of crime, sinful lives resulting in seizure by the Devil and entry into Hell, and premonitions – especially precognitive dreams. Therefore, although the early variants of the Winnats Pass murder tale do not mention the precognitive dream suffered by the female victim ('Clara'), which appears e.g. in the online version recounted in chapter 1, that element is consistent with the story's Methodist roots. The first (1806) edition of Tregortha's book was published and printed by the author, a prolific writer of Methodist tracts, but it ran to many subsequent editions – 1808, 1813, 1815, 1824, 1827 and 1835, mostly published by Gleave and Sons, Manchester. (The quotation given here is from the 1827 edition.) Tregortha died in 1821 but his work continued to sell copies.

7. http://www.rewlach.org.uk/Leek100/LkC1.rtf

8. In his later years he appears to have moved to Tealby, near Market Rasen in Lincolnshire; on 8 September 1819 he invited the Revd Mr Everett of Sheffield to preside at the inaugural service for the new chapel in the village, due to be opened on the first Sunday in October of that year (John Rylands Library PLP 73.24/1).

9. If such a confession was made, no record of it has survived. No writings by the Revd Hume can be found in either the archives of the Diocese of Lichfield, which incorporated the benefice of Castleton during the eighteenth century, or the Derbyshire Record Office.

10. During the retreat of the Jacobite army from Derby there were undoubtedly desertions. However, the disposition of the English forces, notably Field Marshal Wade's army on the east of the Pennines and Cumberland's in Cheshire, plus a gathering of troops in Northampton, was well known among the Scots; they had sent out scouts and their intelligence was fairly good. Therefore, the only direction in which they could safely run if they were to evade capture was northwards into the relatively wild lands of the Peak District (cf. Duffy, 2003). The following comment, which appeared in the *Derby Mercury* in 1849, shows that stray Jacobites were remembered in the area. *SINGULAR DISCOVERY.– A few days ago, a man of the name of Davies, of Foolow, near Eyam, in the Peak, was engaged in removing some mining refuse at a mine called the Highrake, near Eyam, when he came in contact with the hilt of a long spear or sword. After having disengaged the weapon, he found the hilt to be real silver, and very massive. The*

weapon being cleaned presented a very beautiful appearance; nearly the whole of the massively ornamented handle of hilt being silver, on which is the motto, surrounding a rose, Honi soit qui mal y pense. *How such an elegant, and valuable weapon, became deposited there is a query; except it was hid there at the time of the Scottish rebellion, as many of the fugitives of the retreat are known to have passed through this locality.* Whether this speculation is true is beside the point; it is probably not (the weapon may have dated from the Civil War of the mid-seventeenth century). What matters is that even as late as the mid-nineteenth century, it was widely assumed that Jacobite deserters had swarmed over the Peak District.

11. http://www.showcaves.com/english/gb/showcaves/Speedwell.html

12. Including jokes, of course; witness the archetypal 'Englishman, Irishman and Scotsman'.

13. Unlike the 'narratemes' of Propp (1968), these 'elements' are not relevant to a typology of narrative structures; this book considers only a single tale. But in the sense that they are 'the smallest units of the story' they are broadly equivalent to Propp's 'narratemes'.

Chapter Three

1. The supposition is implausible but there is no evidence to refute it. Records of Gretna Green marriages are (more or less) complete only after 1795, and the earliest record still extant dates from 1772 (http://www.achievements.co.uk/services/gretna/index.php). It seems that Gretna Green did not become a popular venue for English 'runaway marriages' until late in the eighteenth century. The earliest surviving records of irregular marriages in Scotland actually hail from Portpatrick, Stranraer, Stonykirk and Leswalt, not Gretna, but most of those were Irish (http://www.sog.org.uk/library/intro.shtml).

2. Of course, if the alleged twenty-year interval between the murders and the confession is taken at face value, these timings are equivalent.

3. This is a hand-written account in a quarto notebook. The date on the inside cover is January 1831; subsequent entries in the notebook are dated later in the 1830s.

4. She also copies the attribution to the *Caledonian Mercury*, but without giving the incorrect 1819 date.

5. The Duke of Devonshire, of Chatsworth House, was entitled to any stray horses on the lands over which he exerted control.

6. The Oden Mine (where at least one of the murderers worked – see above) had its own blacksmith, George Berley, during the 1750s

(Rieuwerts, 1976); though the records do not show whether Berley was working there in 1745.

7. The manuscript in question describes the source as 'Derby News April 28', suggesting that the author did not know the name of the local newspaper.

8. It is not, of course; it is one of Tregortha's books (see chapter 2), though it contains material written by Wesley; and the version of the story in that book is virtually identical to the 1785 *Derby Mercury* article.

9. This is a copy of the 1785 *Derby Mercury* article by Hanby held in the British Library. Curiously, that too is labelled '*Derby News*'.

10. That may help to date the manuscript from which this account is taken. Wright (1831) implies that the barn was still intact at the time she wrote her account, but Wood (1843) mentions 'the remains of the barn' (see following chapter), indicating that the structure was no longer intact. Thus, the anonymous manuscript was probably written in the late 1830s or the very early 1840s. Certainly it must post-date 1819.

Chapter Four

1. In a biographical introduction to Wood's *Tales and Traditions of the Peak* (1862), Peter Furniss wrote: '*The father of William Wood was a lead miner of the olden stamp. He owned the cottage in which he resided, rented a small field or two, and kept his cow.*' As in chapter 1, we see that Peak District lead miners were typically small-time farmers.

2. The first issue of this newspaper was produced on 23 July 1842. It went out of existence in the mid twentieth century and was absorbed, along with the *High Peak News*, into the present-day *Buxton Advertiser.*

3. Peter Harrison has drawn my attention to the large number of child graves in St Edmund's churchyard dating from the second half of the nineteenth century. Many of these unfortunate infants died of malnutrition.

4. This number is correct, since it is the fifth of Wood's sketches, but the subsequent episodes of the tale are numbered wrongly (V, VI and VII rather than VI, VII and VIII).

5. There are other nineteenth century references to this quotation but I have not been able to identify the original author.

6. Wood wrote for readers who were thoroughly familiar with the Bible. See *Judges* 4, verses 11-22. Jael (whose name translates as 'wild goat')

was the wife of Heber the Kenite. When Jabin's captain, Sisera, was defeated at Barak, he fled to the tent of Heber. Jael invited him in and gave him milk; she 'carried butter in a lordly dish'. While he slept she drove a wooden pin ('nail') into his head, to fatal effect, a deed commended by the Judge Deborah.

7. As we shall see, he almost apologises for that transparency at the start of the third episode.

8. We recall that Celia Fiennes travelled 685 miles in seven weeks during her side-saddle journey around England. Assuming that she did not travel on Sundays, that gives an average of about 16 miles per day; and as that intrepid lady observed, "all Derbyshire is full of steepe hills", which would have meant a less than average daily distance. Thus, the difference between an eight-mile and a twelve-mile journey was significant given the terrain through which the couple were journeying.

9. If they went via Hathersage, the distance is about eleven miles. The road via Bradwell is indeed about nine miles, but that involves a journey up Middleton Dale, which was very dangerous before it was turnpiked in the 1760s (Dodd and Dodd, 2000). Avoidance of Middleton Dale seems the only rational explanation for the Royal Oak landlord's circuitous choice of route to Peak Forest.

10. Perhaps it was the now-vanished Speedwell Inn, which was at the foot of the Winnats Pass, where the Speedwell Cavern shop now stands. It was the nearest tavern to the Oden Mine and to other lead mines worked by the alleged murderers. Also, it was well outside Castleton itself – which may have suited travellers intent on secrecy. However, this identification is obviously conjectural.

11. Salvatore Rosa (1615-1673) was an Italian baroque painter whose work (and, apparently, life) was colourful and highly extravagant. His paintings tended to be dark and brooding, prefiguring the Gothic Romanticism that had become popular in many quarters by Wood's time.

12. These are presumably the almost identical accounts by Hanby in the *Arminian Magazine* and the *Derby Mercury* of April 1785.

13. Rogerson (1901) agrees; he states that no names that could be those of the couple appear in the Peak Forest marriage registers.

Chapter Five

1. This magazine was published by Richard Keene of Derby, a local entrepreneur and philanthropist who was also a pioneering

Derbyshire photographer. It is now impossible to trace, so although other episodes of Barrow's tale might have been printed, they cannot be found. Flindall (2005) conjectures that 'Charles Barrow' might be a pseudonym. Indeed it might; alternatively, Charles Barrow might have been a relative by marriage of Richard Keene, whose wife's maiden name was Mary Barrow.

2. *So called from Odin, the Saxon God, and worked in the days of our ancestors.* [Barrow's footnote.]

3. This is held every year on Oak Apple Day, 29 May, and is widely believed to derive from Celtic origins.

4. Reduced to the opening clause in the 1883 edition.

5. The north-eastern extremity of Derbyshire, bordering Sheffield. It is not clear why Bradbury supposes this to be the couple's home.

6. The location of this museum is uncertain. Cowen might have meant Cowen House in Castleton, a private museum run by Mr Pennington of Bolton; or the Douglas House Museum, also in Castleton. These establishments no longer exist.

7. Notwithstanding the expertise of Dodd and Dodd, we should remember that 1758 was the date of enactment of the Castleton-Sparrowpit section of the turnpike; construction followed over the next decade. Also, the bodies could not have been thrown into the Speedwell mine shaft, which did not exist until the 1770s.

8. The booklet was entitled 'Allan and Clara, or the Murder in the Winnats, Castleton'. Peter Harrison, who was one of the Speedwell Cavern guides in 1941-43, lent me a copy.

9. There are no trees around the Winnats Pass. We can only marvel that the murderers were sensitive enough to bury their victims holding hands.

10. http://www.peak-experience.org.uk/tourism/explore-the-guides/peak-experience-guides/bloody-peak/attraction-details/Castleton.html?ContentID=106.

Chapter Six

1. To complicate matters, Nicholas Cock had a younger sister called Mary, but she was only ten years old when James Ashton was married so she is unlikely to have been his wife. The older Mary, daughter of Charles and Margaret Cock, was christened on 3 April 1726, so she was the same age as Ashton.

2. Not before time, apparently; their daughter Molly was born on 25 July 1755. This Thomas Hall became George Bradshaw's brother-in-

law when he married Anna, so if 'John Bradshaw' was really George Bradshaw, two of the alleged murderers were related by marriage.

3. It seems that 1774 was a bad year for the Bradshaws of Castleton. In addition to the infant John, three others them were buried: Micah on 17 March, George on 12 June and Joseph on 16 December.

4. This account includes the alleged halt in Stoney Middleton, so Rogerson was familiar with Wood's version of the story.

5. As described in chapter 2, the *Arminian Magazine* was later called the *Methodist Magazine*. It was this label on the side-saddle that first alerted me to the existence of Hanby (1785).

6. Peter Harrison told me that when the pews in St Edmund's were replaced in the 1960s and '70s, he and other local historians found that the ground under the church floor was a veritable charnel house, packed with human skeletons. Understandably, the vicar did not allow samples to be taken for dating purposes, so the remains were replaced *in situ* and now lie under layers of gravel and concrete. The pews had originally been built over graves – including, so tradition alleges, the grave of a royal princess.

7. Once again, I am indebted to Peter Harrison for this assessment.

8. This is confirmed in DRO Q/RP/1/276/3-4 (the relevant Act was 19 Geo. II).

9. A young couple committed suicide in this cave in the early twentieth century, hence the soubriquet. The suggestions offered in this section of the chapter arose – again – during a conversation with Peter Harrison.

10. I am indebted to Stuart Band, archivist for the Chatsworth estate, for this information. Robert Howe, who died in 1810, and Micah Howe, who died in 1825, are recorded as Barmasters (DRO 1432 A/P1 2/1; Heathcote, 2007). The Barmaster was a Crown representative responsible for the administration of mining law and for measuring the meers of lead veins and the ore extracted from them. He presided over the Barmote or Barmoot, the lead miners' court, which was usually held every six months in each liberty and involved a jury (the 'body of the mine') of 12 or 24 people whose duties continued from one sitting of the court for the next. It is worth noting that one of the main roads in Castleton is still called 'How Lane'.

Chapter Seven

1. Aarne first published his classification in 1910; the Russian version of Propp's book dates from 1927.

2. In the introduction to their *Die Deutsche Sagen*, the Brothers Grimm wrote: '*The fairytale (*Märchen*) is more poetic, the legend (*Sage*) is more historical*'. They observed that a legend is attached to a real locality, and often to known historical persons, in contrast to the fantasy locations and imaginary princesses and giants of a Wonder Tale. See the translation by Ward (1981).

3. See the entries 'legend' and 'local legend' in Simpson and Roud (2003).

4. *Naturphilosophie*. The term was first used by Friedrich von Schelling (1775-1854), who took issue with Immanuel Kant's failure to explain how a free, knowing, non-determined subject (the observer) can arise from a Nature that is wholly governed by deterministic laws, as per Enlightenment philosophy. Schelling attempted to resolve this problem by asserting that Nature – including ourselves as observers – constitutes one complete and self-forming unity, with an innate organising principle that struggles towards self-consciousness.

5. Hence the morpheme 'folk' in *folktale, folklore*, etc. The English word 'folklore' is said to have been invented by a pioneer of English research into 'popular antiquities' and myths, William Thoms (1803-1885), in a letter to *The Athenian* in 1846. Thoms was a great admirer of the German folklorists, particularly Jacob Grimm.

6. Outside the profession of linguistics, of course, Grimm and his brother Wilhelm are best known as collectors and compilers of German Wonder Tales.

7. Olrik (1992, pp. 62-63) wrote: '*The defective forms that come into existence... will most often soon die out. ... There will always be a "struggle for existence" among narratives. More narratives are heard than can be held in one's memory... For this reason alone, a* selection *among the available narratives will constantly take place. The narratives that create the clearest imaginative picture and whose plots aim at definite and universal goals receive preference*' (Olrik's emphasis). The great English folksong collector Cecil J. Sharp held a similar view.

8. Penfield himself was initially responsible for the misrepresentation, writing – almost in the spirit of Freud: '*It is clear that the neuronal action that accompanies each succeeding state of consciousness leaves its permanent imprint on the brain. The imprint, or record, is a trail of facilitation of neuronal connections that can be followed again by an electric current many years later with no loss of detail, as though a tape recorder had been receiving it all*'. In fact, however, memory recovery was observed in just 40 of the 1,132 cases that Penfield examined, and in only about 3 per cent of the total was the recall lifelike and reliable. That is scarcely a basis for a general conclusion.

9. The word was not new: the developmental psychologist Jean Piaget had used it, in much the same sense, as early as 1926, and it was subsequently used by the educational psychologist R. C. Anderson. But Bartlett's application of the idea to *memory for stories* is especially relevant to the present book.

10. The study (presaged in a paper published by Allport and Postman in 1945) is frequently cited, but because most authors who refer to it rely on secondary literature sources rather than the original publication, it is often misinterpreted. In particular, it is often cited as evidence for the unreliability of eye-witness reports, not as a study of the spread of rumours and other oral narratives. This amusing irony, which shows that misinformation can spread as easily through the academic community as through any other, has been pointed out e.g. by Treadway and McCloskey (1987).

11. At least, this seemed to be true of children who had grasped the notion of 'causality'. Those who did not understand causal relationships showed no significant sex difference. Comparing Hutchinson (1809) with Wright (1831), we find that what Freeland and Scholnick (1987) showed in the case of young children might also apply to adults. Although Hutchinson was largely faithful to Hanby's original, he showed a willingness to elaborate the narrative. Wright, however, merely added three explanatory footnotes to the 1829 *Derby Mercury* article, which is essentially similar to Hanby's original (Appendix I), and then reported the apparently 'well-structured' accounts given to her by Mr Eyre and Miss Bradshaw.

12. Imagery, for example, is tied to the visual system, whereas the verbal system seems to work quite differently.

13. Rubin (1995) and many others have used the word 'schema' to denote the thematic plot of a story as well as its mental representation. We need to be clear that a 'schema' is a *mental* entity. It belongs to Popper's World 2, not World 3.

14. As Olrik expressed it: '*moving from calm to excitement, and after the concluding event, in which a principal character frequently has a catastrophe, the Sage ends by moving from excitement to calm*'.

15. '*A hero tries three times to ride up the glass mountain. Three would-be lovers are magically rendered immobile in one night by a maiden ...*'

16. The story grammar – a system of abstract rules for describing the structural regularities of a text – needs to be distinguished from the schema, which is a set of mental expectations about the way in which the story proceeds. Schema and grammar are closely related – one reflects the other – but it is misleading to identify them. In a subsequent paper, Rumelhart wrote: '*A schema is an abstract representation*

of a generic concept for an object, event, or situation. Internally, a schema consists of a network of interrelationships among the major constituents of the situation represented by the schema'. Similarly, Mandler and Johnson (1977) wrote: '*We will use the term 'story schema' to refer to a set of expectations about the internal structure of stories which serves to facilitate both encoding and retrieval'.*

17. On the other hand, in the 'problem-solving story' rules specified by Rumelhart (1975), e.g. ATTEMPT => PLAN + APPLICATION. APPLICATION => PREACTION + ACTION + CONSEQUENCE, the '+' sign is indeed a valid indicator of sequence.

18. In purely formal terms, a non-story would be recognised because it violated the rules of the grammar. However, no grammar proposed so far is either explicit or complete enough to provide such a test. Artificial examples of non-stories have been constructed that can be perceived as non-stories even without consulting a grammar (though the perception could depend on an audience's disposition, not just on the surface text).

19. Mandler cites Propp, but not earlier folklorists. Moreover, she cites Bartlett only in passing, and Allport and Postman not at all.

Appendix II

1. In theory, tithes were payable on (i) all things arising from the ground and subject to annual increase – grain, wood, vegetables etc.; (ii) all things nourished by the ground – the young of cattle, sheep etc., and animal produce such as milk, eggs and wool; and (iii) the produce of man's labour, particularly the profits from mills and fishing. Such tithes were termed respectively predial, mixed and personal tithes. After the Dissolution of the Monasteries, and especially after the enclosures, arrangements for tithes changed greatly and local landowners as well as the clergy profited from them.

References

Aarne, Antti and Thompson, Stith (1995) *The Types of the Folktale: A Classification*, 2nd revised edition. Indiana University Press, Bloomington, IN.

Addy, Sidney O. (1973; original 1895a) *Folk Tales and Superstitions*. E. P. Publishing, Wakefield.

Addy, Sidney O. (1895b) *Household Tales with Other Traditional Remains*. David Nutt, London.

Addy, Sidney O. (1901) 'Garland day at Castleton,' *Folk-lore* 12, 394-428.

Allport, Gordon W. and Postman, Leo (1947) *The Psychology of Rumor*. Henry Holt, New York.

Andrews, Mary (1948) *Long Ago in Peakland*. R. Milward & Sons, Nottingham, pp. 43-44.

Armitage, Jill (2008) *Romantic Haunts of Derbyshire*. Tempus Publishing, Stroud, pp. 46-47.

Ashliman, D. L. (1987) *A Guide to Folktales in the English Language: Based on the Aarne-Thompson Classification System*. Bibliographies and Indexes in World Literature. Greenwood Press, Santa Barbara, CA.

Bagshawe, William H. G. (1887) *A Memoir of William Bagshawe of Ford Hall, styled 'The Apostle of the Peak'*. Mitchell and Hughes, London.

Barnard, Frederick M. (1965). *Herder's Social and Political Thought.* Oxford University Press, Oxford.

Barrow, Charles A. (1857) 'Ellen, a story of the Wyndgates, Derbyshire; Part I,' *The Monthly Penny Magazine* 14, September issue. Derby Local Studies Library, Derbyshire Collection 3212, p. 76.

Bartlett, Frederick C. (1932) *Remembering.* Cambridge University Press, Cambridge.

Bell, David (1993) *Derbyshire Ghosts and Legends.* Countryside Books, Newbury, pp. 24-26.

Belmont, Nicole (1979) *Arnold Van Gennep. The Creator of French Ethnography.* University of Chicago Press, Chicago.

Ben-Amos, Dan (1983) 'The Idea of Folklore: an Essay,' in Ben-Ami, Issachar and Dan, Joseph (eds.) *Studies in Aggadah and Jewish Folklore.* Folklore Research Center Studies VII. Magnes Press, Jerusalem, pp. 11-17.

Bernstein, D. M., Whittlesea, B. W. A. and Loftus, E. F. (2002) 'Increasing confidence in remote autobiographical memory and general knowledge: extensions of the revelation effect,' *Memory and Cognition* 30, 432–438.

Binney, Alfred (1860) 'The late Mr Elias Hall, the geologist,' *Transactions of the Manchester Geological Society* 3, 92-96.

Black's Tourist Guide to Derbyshire, its Towns, Watering Places, Dales and Mountains (1866). Adam and Charles Black, Edinburgh, p. 77.

Bogart, Dan (2004) 'Turnpike trusts and the transportation revolution in 18th century England,' *Explorations in Economic History* 42(4), 479-508.

Bradbury, Edward (1884) *All About Derbyshire.* Simpkin, Marshall & Co., London, pp. 201-202.

Bray, William (1783) *Sketch of a Tour into Derbyshire and Yorkshire,* 2nd edition. B. White, London, p. 189.

Briggs, Katharine M. (1971) *A Dictionary of British Folk-Tales in the English Language*, Part B. Routledge & Kegan Paul, London.

Brooksbanks, Revd James H. (1925) 'Castleton: its traditions, sayings, place names, etc.,' *Transactions of the Hunter Archaeological Society* 3(1), 34-52.

Camden, William (1610) *Britannia*. Bishop and Norton, London.

Childs, Joy (1987) *A History of Derbyshire*. Phillimore and Co., Chichester, p. 85.

Christian, Roy (1996) *Derbyshire Life* 61, pp. 54-59.

Clarke, David (1991) *Ghosts and Legends of the Peak District*. Jarrold Publishing, Norwich, pp. 93-94.

Cocchiara, Giuseppe (1981) *The History of Folklore in Europe*. Institute for the Study of Human Issues, Philadelphia.

Coke, Thomas (1786-8) Letters to Thomas Hanby. John Rylands Library PLP 28.6/10-12.

Colby, Benjamin N. (1973) 'A partial grammar of Eskimo folktales,' *American Anthropologist* 75, 645-662.

Cotton, Charles (1683) *The Wonders of the Peake*. Printed by J. Wallis for Joanna Brome, London.

Cowen, Thomas E. (1910) *History of the Village of Stoney Middleton*, 222. genuki.org.uk/big/eng/DBY/StoneyMiddleton/Cowen, p. 27. Accessed 14/11/08.

Cox, Revd J. Charles (1880) 'The Diary of Edward Bagshawe, Vicar of Castleton, 1723-1769,' *Derbyshire Archaeological Journal* 2, 78-89.

Croston, James (1868) *On Foot through the Peak*, 2nd edition. Simpkin, Marshall & Co., London, p. 16.

Dalrymple, Christina F. (1978) 'The flow of crisis information as a probe of work relations,' *Cahiers Canadiens de Sociologie* 3, 71-88.

Davies, Revd D. P. (1811) *A New Historical and Descriptive View of Derbyshire, from the Remotest Period to the Present Time*, Vol. II. S. Mason, Belper, p. 680 footnote.

Davies, Owen (2002) 'Methodism, the clergy, and popular belief in witchcraft and magic,' *History* 82(266), 252-265.

Defoe, Daniel (1724-6), ed. Rodgers, Pat (1978) *A Tour through the Whole Island of Great Britain*; Vol. III, Letter 8, Part 2. Penguin Classics, Harmondsworth.

Derby and Chesterfield Reporter, 9 February 1832, p. 64, col. 1.

Derby Mercury 17 November 1758, p. 3, col. 2.

Derby Mercury 4 February 1829 p. 2, col. 3.

Derby Mercury 1 August 1849, p. 3, col. 3.

Derby Mercury 21 February 1883 p. 6, col. 5.

Derbyshire Record Office D1154 G/L 4-5, Mine owners and miners, Castleton Liberty 1752-61 and 1761-78.

Derbyshire Record Office D1432 A/P1/1/1-2, Castleton Parish Register, eighteenth century; 1432 A/P1 2/1, nineteenth century.

Derbyshire Record Office D1435 A/P1, Stoney Middleton Parish Register, eighteenth century.

Derbyshire Record Office D1828 A/P1/1/1-3, Hope Parish Register 1661-1736 and 1736-1812.

Derbyshire Record Office D1877/2/9/1, Register of Trust Deeds of Property for Bradwell Circuit, Methodist Church.

Derbyshire Record Office D911Z /P1-2, Survey of the Township of Castleton in the County of Derby, 1819.

Derbyshire Record Office Q/RP/1/276/3-4, Plans of lands and partition of commons, Castleton Parish, 1691; and Sheffield Road Acts, 1758 ff.

Dodd, A. E. and Dodd, E. M. (2000) *Peakland Road and Trackways*. Landmark Publishing, Ashbourne.

Drayton, Michael (1622) *Poly-Olbion Or a Choreographical Description of Tracts, Riuers, Mountaines, Forests and other Parts of this renowned Isle of Great Britaine*. Printed for Iohn Marriott, Iohn Grismand, and Thomas Dewe, London. Song 26, pp. 123-124.

Duffy, Christopher (2003) *The '45: Bonnie Prince Charlie and the Untold Story of the Jacobite Rising*. Cassell, London.

Eisenberg, Elizabeth (1992) *Tales of Old Derbyshire*. Countryside Books, Newbury, pp. 19-22.

Evans, Seth (1907) *Methodism in Bradwell: Work and Worthies of 160 Years*. Chapel Centenary Souvenir. G. H. Bailey, New Mills, pp. 10-29.

Farey, John (1813) *General View of the Agriculture of Derbyshire, with Observations on the Means of its Improvement*. Report to the Board of Agriculture, McMillan, London.

Flindall, Roger (2005) 'Mines, quarries and murders in the Peak District: a study of suspicious deaths and human remains associated with past mineral working activities.' Special issue of the *Bulletin of the Peak District Mines Historical Society: Mining History* 16(1); Peak District Mines Historical Society, Matlock Bath, pp. 17-21.

Foley, John M. (1988) *The Theory of Oral Composition. History and Methodology*. Indiana University Press, Bloomington, IN.

Ford, Trevor D. and Rieuwerts, James H. (1968) *Lead Mining in the Peak District*. Peak Park Planning Board, Bakewell.

Ford, Trevor D. and Rieuwerts, James H. (1976) 'Odin Mine, Castleton, Derbyshire,' *Bulletin of the Peak District Mines Historical Society* 6(4).

Fransella, F. and Bannister, D. (1986) *Inquiring Man: the Theory of Personal Constructs*, 2nd edition. Routledge, London.

Freeland, Claire A. B. and Scholnik, Ellin K. (1987) 'The role of causality in young children's memory for stories,' *International Journal of Behavioral Development* 10(1), 76-88.

Friedman, David (1995) 'Making sense of English law enforcement in the 18ᵗʰ century,' http://www.daviddfriedman.com/Academic/England_18thc./England_18thc.html. Accessed 16/1/09.

Gamer, Michael (2006) *Romanticism and the Gothic. Genre, Reception and Canon Formation*. Cambridge University Press, Cambridge.

Georges, Robert A. and Jones, Michael Owen (1995) *Folkloristics: an Introduction*. Indiana University Press, Bloomington, IN.

Gilchrist, R. Murray (1925) *The Peak District*. Blackie & Sons Ltd., London and Glasgow, p. 52.

Hanby, Thomas (1785) 'A Remarkable PUNISHMENT of MURDER,' *Arminian Magazine*, April issue, 213-214.

Hanby, Thomas (1754-96) Letters. John Rylands Library PLP 48.55.

Harmon, Nolan B. (ed.) (1974) *The Encyclopedia of World Methodism*. United Methodist Publishing House, Nashville. Vol. I, p. 1067.

Harris, Roy and Taylor, Talbot J. (1997) *Landmarks in Linguistic Thought I. The Western Tradition from Socrates to Saussure*. Routledge History of Linguistic Thought Series. Routledge, London (see especially pp. 187-195).

Harrison, Peter C. (2008) *A History of Castleton, and Things Remembered*. Private printing, Castleton.

Heathcote, Chris (2007) 'A gazetteer of the lead mines within Castleton and Hope liberties, Derbyshire: 1748-1898.' *Mining History* 16(6), 1-30; Peak District Mines Historical Society, Matlock Bath.

Hicklin, John and Wallis, Alfred (1872) *Bemrose's Guide to Derbyshire*. Bemrose & Sons, Derby and Matlock Bath, p. 207.

Hobbes, Thomas (1668) *De Mirabilibus Pecci: Wonders of the Peak in Darby-shire*. William Crook, London.

Hope Moncrieff, A. R. (1927) *Derbyshire*. Adam and Charles Black Ltd., London, pp. 38-39.

http://ashbourne-methodist-church.supanet.com/Methodism%20in%20 Ashbourne.html. Accessed 2/12/08.

http://bygonederbyshire.co.uk/articles/Castleton:_Winnat's_Pass,_The_ Ghosts_of_Allan_and_Clara. Accessed 8/11/08.

http://en.wikipedia.org/wiki/Marriage_Act_1753. Accessed 26/11/08.

http://www.achievements.co.uk/services/gretna/index.php. Accessed 15/1/09.

http://www.allsaintsjakarta.org/18centhist.htm, 'The 18th Century Evangelical Revival'. All Saints Resources. Accessed 19/12/08.

http://www.archive.org/stream/norfolkstreetwesooseed/ norfolkstreetwesooseed_djvu.txt. Accessed 11/12/08.

http://www.ashbourne-town.com/history/buildings/zion/zion.html. Accessed 2/12/08.

http://www.peak-experience.org.uk/tourism/explore-the-guides/ peak-experience-guides/bloody-peak/attraction-details/Castleton. html?ContentID=106. Accessed 14/1/09.

http://www.rewlach.org.uk/Leek100/LkC1.rtf. Accessed 2/12/08.

http://www.sheffieldforum.co.uk/showthread.php?t=235866. Accessed 8/11/08.

http://www.showcaves.com/english/gb/showcaves/Speedwell.html. Accessed 5/12/08.

http://www.sog.org.uk/library/intro.shtml. Accessed 15/1/09.

http://www.the-ghosthunters.co.uk/haunted_locations_pg2.html. Accessed 28/05/010

http://www.zurichmansion.org/parks/winnats.html. Accessed 8/11/08.

Hutchinson, John (1809) Hutchinson's Tour through the High Peak of Derbyshire. J. Wilson, Macclesfield, pp. 45-48.

Hutchinson, John (1810) The Stranger at Castleton. Stockport (no publisher named).

Hutton, William; ed. Hunter, Catherine (1816) The Life of William Hutton F.A.S.S., Written by Himself. Beilby & Knotts, Birmingham. www.geocities.com/Nashville/Opry/2848/hutton/life1785.html. Accessed 14/11/08.

Jackson, Thomas (ed.) (2004) Lives of the Early Methodist Preachers, Kessinger, Whitefish, MT. Vol. II, pp. 131-157.

Jewitt, Arthur G. (1811) The History of Buxton; and Visitor's Guide to the Curiosities of the Peak. Private printing, Buxton, p. 110.

Jewitt, Arthur G. (1815) 'Henry and Clara: a Peak Ballad,' in The Wanderings of Memory, or Buxton and the Peak. A Poem: in Three Parts. Printed by W. Marrat, Lincoln, pp. 95-104.

Jewitt, Llewellyn F. W. (1867) The Ballads and Songs of Derbyshire. Bemrose and Lothian, London, pp. 274-275.

Johnson, Nancy and Mandler, Jean M. (1980) A tale of two structures: underlying and surface forms in stories. Poetics 9: 51-86.

Kirshenblatt-Gimblett, Barbara (1996) 'Topic drift. Negotiating the gap between the field and our name,' Journal of Folklore Research 33, 245-254.

Krapf, Norbert (1988) Beneath the Cherry Sapling: Legends from Franconia. Fordham University Press, New York.

Labov, William and Waletzky, Joshua (1967) Narrative analysis: Oral versions of personal experience. In: Helm, June, ed., Essays on the Verbal and Visual Arts. University of Washington Press, Seattle, pp. 12-44.

Langham, Mike and Wells, Colin (1993) Buxton: A Pictorial History. Phillimore, Sussex.

Leach, John T. (1985) Methodism in Buxton. J. T. Leach, private printing, Buxton.

Lewis, Donald M. (1995) The Blackwell Dictionary of Evangelical Biography 1739-1860. Blackwell, Oxford. Vol. 1, p. 513.

Loftus, Elizabeth F. and Loftus, Geoffrey R. (1980) 'On the permanence of stored information in the human brain,' American Psychologist 35, 409–420.

Mandler, Jean M. (1984) Stories, Scripts and Scenes: Aspects of Schema Theory. Erlbaum, Hillsdale, NJ.

Mandler, Jean M. and Johnson, Nancy (1977) Remembrance of things parsed: story structure and recall. Cognitive Psychology 9, 111-151.

Marshall, Thomas, account book for 1785-6. Derby Local Studies Library, MS 9237 052 No. 106.

Marshall, Thomas (1819) Letter to Revd Mr Everett. John Rylands Library PLP 73.24/1.

McCann, Andrew (ed.) (1999) The History and Antiquities of Eyam by William Wood (1842, 1845 & 1860). Country Books, Little Longstone.

Merrill, John N. (1975) Legends of Derbyshire, 2nd edition. Dalesman Publishing Co., Clapham, pp. 23-26.

Morpurgo Davies, Anna (1987) '"Organic" and "Organicism" in Franz Bopp,' in Hoenigswald, Henry M. and Wiener, Linda F. (eds.) Biological Metaphor and Cladistic Classification. An Interdisciplinary Perspective. University of Pennsylvania Press, Philadephia, pp. 81-108.

Morris, C. (1982) The Illustrated Journeys of Celia Fiennes 1685-c.1712. MacDonald and Co., London and Sydney, pp. 104-107.

Nicholson, William (1812) 'Models of all the most interesting parts of the High Peak of Derbyshire,' Journal of Natural Philosophy, Chemistry and the Arts 23, 226-228.

Ogle, Revd Alan (1998) 'Methodism in the Peak'. Articles in The Link (Peak Methodist Circuit Magazine), pp. 6-8, 12-15.

Olrik, Axel (1965). 'Epic Laws of Folk Narrative'. In Dundes, Alan (ed.) The Study of Folklore. Prentice-Hall, Englewood Cliffs, NJ, pp. 129-141.

Olrik, Axel (1992) Principles for Oral Narrative Research. Folklore Studies in Translation. Indiana University Press, Bloomington, IN.

Olsen, Kirstin (1999) Daily Life in 18th-Century England. Greenwood Press, Westport, CT.

Ousby, I. (ed.) (1992) James Plumptre's Britain: the Journals of a Tourist in the 1790s. Random Century Group, London, pp. 67-71.

Peak National Park Information Section (1975) The Winnats. Leaflet printed by Derwent Press Ltd., Derby.

Penfield, Wilder (1952) Memory Mechanisms. AMA Archives of Neurology and Psychiatry 67, 178-198.

Philip, Neil (1993) The Penguin Book of English Folktales. Penguin, Harmondsworth.

Pilkington. J. (1789) A View of the Present State of Derbyshire. J. Drewry, Derby vol. I, pp. 76-77.

Pill, A. L. (1949) 'Eldon Hole in romance and reality,' Derbyshire Countryside 17(5), 240-241.

Popper, Karl R. (1978) 'Three worlds.' The Tanner Lecture on Human Values. http://www.tannerlectures.utah.edu/lectures/atoz.html#p. Accessed 12/4/08.

Propp, L. Vladimir (orig. 1927, trans. 1968) Morphology of the Folktale, translated by Scott, Laurence. University of Texas Press, Austin, TX.

Rawlinson, R. (1954) 'A saddle with a history.' Derbyshire Countryside 20(2), 37.

Rhodes, Ebenezer (1824) Peak Scenery, or Excursions in Derbyshire made Chiefly for the Purpose of Picturesque Observation. Longman, Hurst, Rees, Orme, Brown and Green, London.

Rhodes, John (1973) Derbyshire Lead Mining in the Eighteenth Century. University of Sheffield Institute of Education.

Richards, R. (2002) The Romantic Conception of Life: Science and Philosophy in the Age of Goethe. University of Chicago Press, Chicago.

Rieuwerts, James H. (1965) 'The Odin, one of Derbyshire's oldest mines,' Derbyshire Life and Countryside 30(3), 55-57.

Rieuwerts, James H. (1972) Derbyshire's Old Lead Mines and Miners. Moorland Publishing, Kettering.

Rieuwerts, James H. (1976) 'The history of the Odin Mine,' Peak District Mines Historical Society Bulletin 6(4), 7-29.

Rippon, Anton (1982) Folktales and Legends of Derbyshire. Minimax, Peterborough, pp. 52-55.

Robertson, William H. (1872) A Handbook to the Peak of Derbyshire and to the Use of the Buxton Mineral Waters; or, Buxton in 1854. Bradbury and Evans, London.

Rogerson, Revd George (1901) Preface; in Marshall, George W. (ed.) The Marriage Registers of Peak Forest Chapel. Private printing, Worksop.

Rubin, David C. (1995) Memory in Oral Traditions: The Cognitive Psychology of Epic, Ballads, and Counting-out Rhymes. Oxford University Press, New York.

Rumelhart, David (1977) Understanding and summarizing brief stories. In: LaBerge, David and Samuels, Jay, eds., Basic Processes in Reading: Perception and Comprehension. Erlbaum, Hillsdale, NJ, pp. 265-303.

Schacter, Daniel L. (ed.) (1995) Memory Distortion. Harvard University Press, Cambridge, MA.

Sewell, Anna (1811) Letters Written between the Years 1784-1807. Private printing, Edinburgh.

Shawcross, Revd William H. (1903) Some Notices of Castleton and its Old Inhabitants from AD 1645 to AD 1837. C. E. Turner, Hemsworth.

Sheffield City Archives, Bag C/315 (the diary or commonplace book of the Revd Edward Bagshawe, Vicar of Castleton). Ac. No. 40191.

Sheffield City Archives, Bag C/3363/11 (anonymous and undated account of the murders).

Sampson, Georgiana R. (1921) Herder's Conception of 'das Volk'. University of Chicago Libraries, Chicago.

Simpson, Jacqueline (1991) The Local Legend: a product of popular culture. Rural History 2, 25-35.

Simpson, Jacqueline and Roud, Steve (2003) A Dictionary of English Folklore. Oxford University Press, Oxford.

Smith, Roland (2004) Murder and Mystery in the Peak. Halsgrove, Tiverton, pp. 33-35.

Stevens, David (2000) The Gothic Tradition. Cambridge University Press, Cambridge.

Tangherlini, Timothy R. (1990) 'It Happened Not Too Far from Here ...': A Survey of Legend Theory and Characterization. Western Folklore 49, 371-390.

Taylor, John (1618) The Pennyles Pilgrimage, or The Money-Lesse Perambulation. Printed for the author by Edward Allde, London.

Thompson, Stith 1946: The Folktale. University of California Press, Berkeley.

Thorndyke, Perry (1977) Cognitive structures in comprehension and memory of narrative discourse. Cognitive Psychology 9, 77-110.

Tolkien, John R. R. (1939) 'On Fairy-Stories'. Andrew Lang Lecture, University of St Andrews. Republished (1964) in Tree and Leaf, George Allen and Unwin, London.

Tomlinson, Tom D. (1985) Travel in the Hope Valley 2000BC-2000AD. Valley Printers, Hathersage.

Treadway, Molly and McCloskey, Michael (1987) 'Distortions of the Allport and Postman rumor study in the eyewitness testimony literature,' Law and Human Behavior 11, 19-25.

Tregortha, John (1827; original 1806) *News from the Invisible World; or, Interesting Anecdotes of the Dead*. Published by the author, Burslem. Later editions (e.g. 1827) published by J. Gleave and Sons, Manchester.

Turner, William M. (1901) *Romances of the Peak*. Simpkin, Marshall & Co., London.

Uther, Hans-Jörg (2004) *The Types of International Folktales: a Classification and Bibliography Based on the System of Antti Aarne and Stith Thompson*. Academia Scientiarum Fennica, Helsinki.

Viëtor, Karl (1950) *Goethe the Thinker*. Harvard University Press, Cambridge MA.

von Sydow, Carl W. (1948) *Selected Papers on Folklore. Published on the Occasion of his 70th Birthday*. Rosenkilde and Bagger, Copenhagen.

Ward, Donald (1981) *The German Legends of the Brothers Grimm*. Institute for the Study of Human Issues, Philadelphia, PA.

Ward, W. Reginald (1992) *The Protestant Evangelical Awakening*. Cambridge University Press, New York.

Westwood, Jennifer (1987) *Albion: Guide to Legendary Britain*, 2nd edition. Grafton, London.

Westwood, Jennifer and Simpson, Jacqueline (2006) *The Lore of the Land*. Penguin, London.

Whitehead, A. N. (1925) *Science and the Modern World*. Macmillan, New York.

Williams, Ethel C. (1947) *Companion into Derbyshire*. Methuen & Co. Ltd., London, p. 8.

Wolley Manuscript (1788), British Museum 6668 f.470.

Wood, William (1843) 'Historical and descriptive sketches of Buxton and its vicinity, IV-VII,' *Buxton Herald and Gazette of Fashion* 20(2), July 13, p. 3, col 1; 21(2), July 20, p. 3, col. 1-2; 22(2) July 27, p. 3, col. 1-2; 23(2) August 3, p. 3, col. 1-2.

Wood, William (1862) 'Allan and Clara: or the Murder in the Winnats, Castleton.' In *Tales and Traditions of the High Peak*, Bell and Daldy, London, pp. 34-58. (This chapter was also published separately, anonymously and undated, by J. Smith and Sons, Bakewell.)

Wright, Hannah (1831) 'Traditions, Occurrences, &c., in the Neighbourhood of Hathersage,' *Derbyshire Record Office* D5776/2, MS 9564, pp. 1-6.

Also Available From
Amberley Publishing

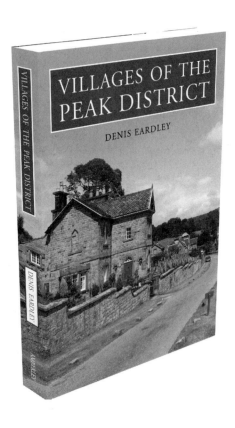

Villages of
the Peak District

Denis Eardley

Price: £16.99
ISBN: 978-1-84868-728-8
Binding: PB
Extent: 256 pages

Available from all good bookshops or order direct
from our website www.amberleybooks.com